1 3 5 7 9 10 8 6 4 2

Vintage
20 Vauxhall Bridge Road,
London SW1V 2SA

Vintage Classics is part of the Penguin Random House group of companies whose addresses can be found at global.penguinrandomhouse.com

Penguin Random House UK

The essay 'We Are Double-Plus Unfree' was first published in the United Kingdom in the *Guardian* in 2015
The Handmaid's Tale was first published in the United Kingdom by Jonathan Cape in 1986
Hag-Seed was first published in the United Kingdom by Hogarth in 2016
This short edition published by Vintage in 2018

penguin.co.uk/vintage

A CIP catalogue record for this book is available from the British Library

ISBN 9781784874117

Typeset in 9.5/14.5 pt FreightText Pro
by Jouve (UK), Milton Keynes
Printed and bound by Clays Ltd, St Ives plc

Freedom

MARGARET ATWOOD

VINTAGE MINIS

We Are Double-Plus Unfree

'A ROBIN REDBREAST in a cage, Puts all Heaven in a Rage,' wrote William Blake. 'Sufficient to have stood, though free to fall,' wrote John Milton, channelling God's musings about mankind and free will in the third book of *Paradise Lost*. 'Freedom, high-day, high-day, freedom . . . !' chants Caliban in *The Tempest*. Mind you, he is drunk at the time, and overly optimistic: the choice he is making is not freedom, but subjection to a tyrant.

We're always talking about it, this 'freedom'. But what do we mean by it? 'There is more than one kind of freedom,' Aunt Lydia lectures the captive Handmaids in my 1985 novel, *The Handmaid's Tale*. 'Freedom to and freedom from. In the days of anarchy, it was freedom to. Now you are being given freedom from. Don't underrate it.'

The robin redbreast is safer in the cage: it won't get eaten by cats or smash into windows. It will have lots to eat. But it will also not be able to fly wherever it likes. Presumably this is what troubles the inhabitants of heaven:

they object to the restriction placed on the flight options of a fellow winged being. The robin should live in nature, where it belongs: it should have 'freedom to', the active mode, rather than 'freedom from', the passive mode.

That's all very well for robins. Hooray for Blake, we say! But what about us? Should we choose 'freedom from' or 'freedom to'? The safe cage or the dangerous wild? Comfort, inertia and boredom, or activity, risk and peril? Being human and therefore of mixed motives, we want both; though, as a rule, alternately. Sometimes the desire for risk leads to boundary-crossing and criminal activity, and sometimes the craving for safety leads to self-imprisonment.

Governments know our desire for safety all too well, and like to play on our fears. How often have we been told that this or that new rule or law or snooping activity on the part of officialdom is to keep us 'safe'? We aren't safe, anyway: many of us die in weather events – tornados, floods, blizzards – but governments, in those cases, limit their roles to finger-pointing, blame-dodging, expressions of sympathy or a dribble of emergency aid. Many more of us die in car accidents or from slipping in the bathtub than are likely to be done in by enemy agents, but those kinds of deaths are not easy to leverage into panic. Cars and bathtubs are so recent in evolutionary terms that we've developed no deep mythology about them. When coupled with human beings of ill intent they can be scary – being rammed in your car by a maniac or shot in your car by a mafioso carry a certain weight, and being slaughtered in the tub goes back to Agamemnon's fate in Homer, with a shower-murder update courtesy of Alfred Hitchcock in his film *Psycho*. But cars and tubs minus enraged wives or maniacs just sit there blankly.

It's the sudden, violent, unpredictable event we truly fear: the equivalent of an attack by a hungry tiger. Yesterday's frightful tigerish threat was communists: in the 1950s, one lurked in every shrub, ran the message. Today, it's terrorists. To protect us from these, all sorts of precautions must, we are told, be taken. Nor is this view without merit: such threats are real, up to a point. Nonetheless we find ourselves asking whether the extreme remedies outweigh the disease. How much of our own freedom must we sacrifice in order to defend ourselves against the desire of others to limit that freedom by subjugating or killing us, one by one?

And is that sacrifice an effective defence? Minus our freedom, we may find ourselves no safer; indeed we may be double-plus unfree, having handed the keys to those who promised to be our defenders but who have become, perforce, our jailers. A prison might be defined as any place you've been put into against your will and can't get out of, and where you are entirely at the mercy of the authorities, whoever they may be. Are we turning our entire society into a prison? If so, who are the inmates and who are the guards? And who decides?

* * *

We human beings have been exploring the border between freedom and unfreedom for a very long time. Long ago, the alternative to freedom was not imprisonment but death. In the millennia we spent as hunter-gatherers, we had neither passwords nor prisons. Everyone in your small group knew and accepted you, though strangers were suspect. No one got put in jail, because there were no buildings to serve that purpose. If a person became a threat to the group – for instance, if he became psychotic and expressed a desire to eat people – it would be the duty of the group to kill him, whereas nowadays it would be the duty of the group to lock him up, in order to keep others from harm. A justice system with an incarceration option depends on permanent architecture: you can't throw someone into a dungeon unless you have one.

After the advent of agriculture, the alternative to freedom became not death but slavery. It was now more desirable to enslave the threats to your group than to kill them. That way, they could be set to work tilling your soil, thus creating a surplus for you and making you rich. Sampson isn't tossed off a cliff, as were the captured male Trojans in the Homeric epics. Instead he is blinded and set to work grinding grain like a donkey.

Of course, once the profitability of slaves had been recognised, the rule of supply and demand created a thriving market for slaves. You could find yourself enslaved not only by being on the losing end of a war, but by being in the wrong place at the wrong time: in the path of a slave-raiding party, for instance.

In the medieval period, everyone in the upper percentages wanted a castle, and every castle had a dungeon: dark, dismal, cold, hopeless and rat-infested, or such is their filmic image. Dungeons were status symbols: everyone who was anyone had one. They had multiple uses: you could keep witches in them until it was time to burn them; you could shackle criminals in them, though it was often more economical to just hang them; and you could put rivals to the throne in them until you could fabricate enough evidence to proclaim them traitors and chop off their heads. And dungeons could be valuable wealth-creators, since holding foreign nobles for ransom could be lucrative. The trade was simple: you, the dungeon-possessor, got a lump sum of cash, and your prisoner got his freedom. In the reverse version, you paid a foreign dungeon-owner to sequester the political enemy of your choice.

And so it went, for hundreds of years, up to the modern age. In the 19th century, freedom and unfreedom began to assume their present-day forms. 'Freedom' had become reified by the 18th-century Enlightenment: it was what the embattled farmers of the American revolution were supposed to have been fighting for, though in practical terms they were fighting for the freedom of not paying taxes to Britain. The French revolutionaries started out with liberty, equality and fraternity, a noble ideal which included freedom from the aristocrats, though in the short term it ended in tears, thousands of severed heads and Napoleon.

But once Byron got hold of freedom, there was no turning back: freedom as an idea was here to stay. His *The Prisoner of Chillon* was romantic because he didn't have freedom; that dubious character, Fletcher Christian, mutinied against Captain Bligh – in Byron's version – as a gesture against tyranny and a bid for freedom. And Byron himself lost his life while fighting, more or less, for the Greeks in their attempt to regain their own political freedom. Not 'Dieu et mon droit' but 'Freedom' was engraved on the banner waved by many a 19th- and 20th-century revolutionary: slaves' freedom from slavery in the American south, South Americans' freedom from Spain, Russians' freedom from the tsar, workers' freedom from capitalist exploitation, women's freedom from patriarchal systems in which they had the rights of children but the responsibilities of adults. And, eventually, freedom from Nazism and Iron Curtain Communism.

Freedom to write, freedom to publish, freedom of speech: all are still being fought for in many countries in the world. Their martyrs are numerous.

With so many so willing to die in its name, why have citizens in many western countries been willing to surrender their hard-won freedoms with barely more than a squeak? Usually it's fear. And fear can come in many forms: sometimes it comes down to the fear of not having a paycheque. As long as the trains run on time and you yourself are employed, why make a fuss if a few people here and there are being strung up by their thumbs?

And by the time the thumb-stringing really gets going, fear of another kind sets in. You can protect your thumbs only by staying below the surface of the frog pond: don't stick your head up or croak too loudly, and, you are assured, as long as you don't do anything 'wrong' – a shifting category – nothing bad will happen to you.

Until it does.

And since the free press will already have been suppressed, and since any independent judiciary will already have been dismantled, and since any independent writers, singers and artists will already have been squashed, there will be no one left to defend you. If there's one thing we ought to know by now, it's that absolutist systems with no accountability and no checks and balances generate monstrous abuses of power. That seems to be an infallible rule.

But all of that may seem a little old-fashioned. It harks back to the mid-20th century, with its brutalism, its strutting dictators, its mass military spectacles, its crude in-your-face uniforms. The citizen-control methods of modern western governments are much more low-profile: less jackboot than gumboot. Our leaders are applying the methods of agribusiness cattle-raising to us: ear-tag, barcode, number, sort, record. And cull, of course.

That's where the prison system comes in: shorn of its

short-lived idealism – no longer a reformatory where criminals are to be reformed, no longer a penitentiary where they are to repent – it has become a warehouse where people are stashed. In its for-profit mode, it has also become a gizmo for creating more criminals, all the better to fill its available slots and extract money from taxpayers to foot the bill for it.

In the US, young black men are disproportionately represented in the prison population; in Canada, it's young First Nations men. Are we incapable of thinking up anything more effective, and at the same time less costly, such as better education and better job creation? But maybe it serves the powers that be to foster the conditions that create scary people and have them running around, so we ourselves will see the logic of paying to lock them up.

Digital technology has made it easier than ever to treat people like domesticated animals farmed for profit. You can no longer rent a car or a hotel room or buy much of anything without a credit card, which leaves a digital trail wherever it goes. You're told you need a social security card, a health card, a driver's licence, a bank card, a bunch of passwords. You need an 'identity', and that identity is digital. All your numbers and passwords – all the data that identifies you – is supposed to be private, but as we know by now, the digital world leaks like a sieve, and security on the internet is only as good as the next mastermind hacker or inside-job data thief. The Kremlin has gone back to using typewriters for a good reason: it's a lot easier to smuggle a memory stick out of a secure area than it is to make off with a big stack of papers.

So, what to do? In William Gibson's Neuromancer trilogy, most of the citizens are ear-tagged just like us, but some are able to exist under the radar by virtue of having no official record. Either they've wiped it or altered it, or they've avoided having one in the first place. But it would take a lot of agility and possibly a reservoir of basic survival skills for anyone to live without the required identity. Under a bridge, maybe; in a house, not.

The majority of us are double-plus unfree: our 'freedom to' is limited to approved and supervised activities, and our 'freedom from' doesn't keep us free from a great many things that can end up killing us, with our bathtubs being just the beginning. Freedom from toxic chemicals in the air and water? Freedom from floods, droughts and famines? Freedom from defective automobiles? Freedom from the badly prescribed drugs that are killing hundreds of thousands of people a year? Don't hold your breath.

It's not all bad, however. All technology is a double-edged tool, and the very internet that has too many data-leaking holes in it also allows words to travel quickly. It's easier to reveal abuses of power than it once was; it's easier to sign petitions and to protest. Though even that freedom is double-edged: the petition you sign may be used by your own government in evidence against you.

One of Aesop's fables concerns the frogs. They told the gods they wanted a king, and the gods threw down a log to be their ruler. It floated here and there and didn't do anything, and for a while they were content. But then they began complaining, because they wanted a more active king. The gods, annoyed, sent them a stork, which ate them up.

Our problem is that our western governments, increasingly, are an unpleasant combination of both the Log King and the Stork King. They're good at asserting their own freedom to spy and control, though bad at allowing their citizens as much freedom as they formerly enjoyed. Good at devising spy laws, bad at protecting us from the consequences of them, including false positives. Who says you are who you are? Whoever can alter your data.

Though our digital technologies have made life superconvenient for us – just tap and it's yours, whatever it is – maybe it's time for us to recapture some of the territory we've ceded. Time to pull the blinds, exclude the snoops, recapture the notion of privacy. Go offline.

Any volunteers? Right. I thought not. It won't be easy.

Western governments are good at asserting their own freedom to spy and control, though bad at allowing their citizens as much freedom as they formerly enjoyed

From *The Handmaid's Tale*

OFFRED IS A Handmaid in the Republic of Gilead. Her only function is to breed, to bear the child of her Commander on behalf of his wife. If she deviates from her duty, she will, like dissenters, be hanged at the wall or sent out to die slowly of radiation sickness. She chose this life – though the other option was exile to the Colonies. That has been one of her few freedoms in this repressive state where, separated from her husband and daughter, she can trust no one.

One

DOUBLED, I WALK the street. Though we are no longer in the Commanders' compound, there are large houses here also. In front of one of them a Guardian is mowing the lawn. The lawns are tidy, the façades are gracious, in good repair; they're like the beautiful pictures they used to print in the magazines about homes and gardens and interior decoration. There is the same absence of people, the same air of being asleep. The street is almost like a museum, or a street in a model town constructed to show the way people used to live. As in those pictures, those museums, those model towns, there are no children.

This is the heart of Gilead, where the war cannot intrude except on television. Where the edges are we aren't sure, they vary, according to the attacks and counterattacks; but this is the centre, where nothing moves. The Republic of Gilead, said Aunt Lydia, knows no bounds. Gilead is within you.

Doctors lived here once, lawyers, university professors. There are no lawyers any more, and the university is closed.

Luke and I used to walk together, sometimes, along these streets. We used to talk about buying a house like one of these, an old big house, fixing it up. We would have a garden, swings for the children. We would have children. Although we knew it wasn't too likely we could ever afford it, it was something to talk about, a game for Sundays. Such freedom now seems almost weightless.

We turn the corner onto a main street, where there's more traffic. Cars go by, black most of them, some grey and brown. There are other women with baskets, some in red, some in the dull green of the Marthas, some in the striped dresses, red and blue and green and cheap and skimpy, that mark the women of the poorer men. Econowives, they're called. These women are not divided into functions. They have to do everything; if they can. Sometimes there is a woman all in black, a widow. There used to be more of them, but they seem to be diminishing.

You don't see the Commanders' Wives on the sidewalks. Only in cars.

The sidewalks here are cement. Like a child, I avoid stepping on the cracks. I'm remembering my feet on these sidewalks, in the time before, and what I used to wear on them. Sometimes it was shoes for running, with cushioned soles and breathing holes, and stars of fluorescent fabric that reflected light in the darkness. Though I never ran at night; and in the daytime, only beside well-frequented roads.

Women were not protected then.

I remember the rules, rules that were never spelled out but that every woman knew: don't open your door to a stranger, even if he says he is the police. Make him slide his ID under the door. Don't stop on the road to help a motorist pretending to be in trouble. Keep the locks on and keep going. If anyone whistles, don't turn to look. Don't go into a laundromat, by yourself, at night.

I think about laundromats. What I wore to them: shorts, jeans, jogging pants. What I put into them: my own clothes, my own soap, my own money, money I had earned myself. I think about having such control.

Now we walk along the same street, in red pairs, and no man shouts obscenities at us, speaks to us, touches us. No one whistles.

There is more than one kind of freedom, said Aunt Lydia. Freedom to and freedom from. In the days of anarchy, it was freedom to. Now you are being given freedom from. Don't underrate it.

In front of us, to the right, is the store where we order dresses. Some people call them *habits*, a good word for them. Habits are hard to break. The store has a huge wooden sign outside it, in the shape of a golden lily; Lilies of the Field, it's called. You can see the place, under the lily, where the lettering was painted out, when they decided that even the names of shops were too much temptation for us. Now places are known by their signs alone.

Lilies used to be a movie theatre, before. Students went there a lot; every spring they had a Humphrey Bogart festival, with Lauren Bacall or Katherine Hepburn, women on their own, making up their minds. They wore blouses with buttons down the front that suggested the possibilities of the word *undone*. These women could be undone; or not. They seemed to be able to choose. We seemed to be able to choose, then. We were a society dying, said Aunt Lydia, of too much choice.

I don't know when they stopped having the festival. I must have been grown up. So I didn't notice.

We don't go into Lilies, but across the road and along a side-street. Our first stop is at a store with another wooden sign: three eggs, a bee, a cow. Milk and Honey. There's a line, and we wait our turn, two by two. I see they have oranges today. Ever since Central America was lost to the Libertheos, oranges have been hard to get: sometimes they are there, sometimes not. The war interferes with the oranges from California, and even Florida isn't dependable, when there are roadblocks or when the train tracks have been blown up. I look at the oranges, longing for one. But I haven't brought any tokens for oranges. I'll go back and tell Rita about them, I think. She'll be pleased. It will be something, a small achievement, to have made oranges happen.

Those who've reached the counter hand their tokens

across it, to the two men in Guardian uniforms who stand on the other side. Nobody talks much, though there is a rustling, and the women's heads move furtively from side to side: here, shopping, is where you might see someone you know, someone you've known in the time before, or at the Red Centre. Just to catch sight of a face like that is an encouragement. If I could see Moira, just see her, know she still exists. It's hard to imagine now, having a friend.

But Ofglen, beside me, isn't looking. Maybe she doesn't know anyone any more. Maybe they have all vanished, the women she knew. Or maybe she doesn't want to be seen. She stands in silence, head down.

As we wait in our double line, the door opens and two more women come in, both in the red dresses and white wings of the Handmaids. One of them is vastly pregnant; her belly, under her loose garment, swells triumphantly. There is a shifting in the room, a murmur, an escape of breath; despite ourselves we turn our heads, blatantly, to see better; our fingers itch to touch her. She's a magic presence to us, an object of envy and desire, we covet her. She's a flag on a hilltop, showing us what can still be done: we too can be saved.

The women in the room are whispering, almost talking, so great is their excitement.

'Who is it?' I hear behind me.

'Ofwayne. No. Ofwarren.'

'Show-off,' a voice hisses, and this is true. A woman that's pregnant doesn't have to go out, doesn't have to go shopping. The daily walk is no longer prescribed, to keep her abdominal muscles in working order. She needs only the floor exercises, the breathing drill. She could stay at her house. And it's dangerous for her to be out, there must be a Guardian standing outside the door, waiting for her. Now that she's the carrier of life, she is closer to death, and needs special security. Jealousy could get her, it's happened before. All children are wanted now, but not by everyone.

But the walk may be a whim of hers, and they humour whims, when something has gone this far and there's been no miscarriage. Or perhaps she's one of those, *Pile it on, I can take it*, a martyr. I catch a glimpse of her face, as she raises it to look around. The voice behind me was right. She's come to display herself. She's glowing, rosy, she's enjoying every minute of this.

'Quiet,' says one of the Guardians behind the counter, and we hush like schoolgirls.

Ofglen and I have reached the counter. We hand over our tokens, and one Guardian enters the numbers on them into the Compubite while the other gives us our purchases, the milk, the eggs. We put them into our baskets and go out again, past the pregnant woman and her partner, who beside her looks spindly, shrunken; as we all do. The pregnant woman's belly is like a huge fruit. *Humungous*, word of my childhood. Her hands rest on it as if to defend it, or as if they're gathering something from it, warmth and strength.

As I pass she looks full at me, into my eyes, and I know who she is. She was at the Red Centre with me, one of Aunt Lydia's pets. I never liked her. Her name, in the time before, was Janine.

Janine looks at me, then, and around the corners of her mouth there is the trace of a smirk. She glances down to where my own belly lies flat under my red robe, and the wings cover her face. I can see only a little of her forehead, and the pinkish tip of her nose.

NEXT WE GO into All Flesh, which is marked by a large wooden pork chop hanging from two chains. There isn't so much of a line here: meat is expensive, and even the Commanders don't have it every day. Ofglen gets steak, though, and that's the second time this week. I'll tell that to the Marthas: it's the kind of thing they enjoy hearing about. They are very interested in how other households are run; such bits of petty gossip give them an opportunity for pride or discontent.

I take the chicken, wrapped in butcher's paper and trussed with string. Not many things are plastic, any more. I remember those endless white plastic shopping bags, from the supermarket; I hated to waste them and would stuff them in under the sink, until the day would come when there would be too many and I would open the cupboard door and they would bulge out, sliding over the floor. Luke used to complain about it. Periodically he would take all the bags and throw them out.

She could get one of those over her head, he'd say. You know how kids like to play. She never would, I'd say. She's too old. (Or too smart, or too lucky.) But I would feel a chill of fear, and then guilt for having been so careless. It was true, I took too much for granted; I trusted fate, back then. I'll keep them in a higher cupboard, I'd say. Don't keep them at all, he'd say. We never use them for anything. Garbage bags, I'd say. He'd say . . .

Not here and now. Not where people are looking. I turn, see my silhouette in the plate-glass window. We have come outside then, we are on the street.

A GROUP OF people is coming towards us. They're tourists, from Japan it looks like, a trade delegation perhaps, on a tour of the historic landmarks or out for local colour. They're diminutive and neatly turned out; each has his or her camera, his or her smile. They look around, bright-eyed, cocking their heads to one side like robins, their very cheerfulness aggressive, and I can't help staring. It's been a long time since I've seen skirts that short on women. The skirts reach just below the knee and the legs come out from beneath them, nearly naked in their thin stockings, blatant, the high-heeled shoes with their straps attached to the feet like delicate instruments of torture. The women teeter on their spiked feet as if on stilts, but off balance; their backs arch at the waist, thrusting the buttocks out. Their heads are uncovered and their hair too is exposed, in all its darkness and sexuality. They wear lipstick, red, outlining the damp cavities of their mouths, like scrawls on a washroom wall, of the time before.

I stop walking. Ofglen stops beside me and I know that she too cannot take her eyes off these women. We are fascinated, but also repelled. They seem undressed. It has taken so little time to change our minds, about things like this.

Then I think: I used to dress like that. That was freedom.

Westernized, they used to call it.

The Japanese tourists come towards us, twittering, and we turn our heads away too late: our faces have been seen.

There's an interpreter, in the standard blue suit and red-patterned tie, with the winged-eye tie pin. He's the one who steps forward, out of the group, in front of us, blocking our way. The tourists bunch behind him; one of them raises a camera.

'Excuse me,' he says to both of us, politely enough. 'They're asking if they can take your picture.'

I look down at the sidewalk, shake my head for *No*. What they must see is the white wings only, a scrap of face, my chin and part of my mouth. Not the eyes. I know better than to look the interpreter in the face. Most of the interpreters are Eyes, or so it's said.

I also know better than to say Yes. Modesty is invisibility, said Aunt Lydia. Never forget it. To be seen – to be *seen* – is to be – her voice trembled – penetrated. What you must be, girls, is impenetrable. She called us girls.

Beside me, Ofglen is also silent. She's tucked her red-gloved hands up into her sleeves, to hide them.

The interpreter turns back to the group, chatters at them in staccato. I know what he'll be saying, I know the line. He'll be telling them that the women here have different customs, that to stare at them through the lens of a camera is, for them, an experience of violation.

I'm looking down, at the sidewalk, mesmerized by the women's feet. One of them is wearing open-toed sandals, the toenails painted pink. I remember the smell of nail polish, the way it wrinkled if you put the second coat on too soon, the satiny brushing of sheer pantyhose against the skin, the way the toes felt, pushed towards the opening in the shoe by the whole weight of the body. The woman with painted toes shifts from one foot to the other. I can feel her shoes, on my own feet. The smell of nail polish has made me hungry.

'Excuse me,' says the interpreter again, to catch our attention. I nod, to show I've heard him.

'He asks, are you happy,' says the interpreter. I can imagine it, their curiosity: *Are they happy? How can they be happy?* I can feel their bright black eyes on us, the way they lean a little forward to catch our answers, the women especially, but the men too: we are secret, forbidden, we excite them.

Ofglen says nothing. There is a silence. But sometimes it's as dangerous not to speak.

'Yes, we are very happy,' I murmur. I have to say something. What else can I say?

Two

A BLOCK PAST All Flesh, Ofglen pauses, as if hesitant about which way to go. We have a choice. We could go straight back, or we could walk the long way around. We already know which way we will take, because we always take it.

'I'd like to pass by the church,' says Ofglen, as if piously.

'All right,' I say, though I know as well as she does what she's really after.

We walk, sedately. The sun is out, in the sky there are white fluffy clouds, the kind that look like headless sheep. Given our wings, our blinkers, it's hard to look up, hard to get the full view, of the sky, of anything. But we can do it, a little at a time, a quick move of the head, up and down, to the side and back. We have learned to see the world in gasps.

To the right, if you could walk along, there's a street that would take you down towards the river. There's a boathouse, where they kept the sculls once, and some bridges; trees, green banks, where you could sit and watch the water, and the young men with their naked arms, their oars lifting into the sunlight as they played at winning. On the way to the river are the old dormitories, used for something else now, with their fairytale turrets, painted white and gold and blue. When we think of the past it's the beautiful things we pick out. We want to believe it was all like that.

The football stadium is down there too, where they hold the Men's Salvagings. As well as the football games. They still have those.

I don't go to the river any more, or over bridges. Or on the subway, although there's a station right there. We're not allowed on, there are Guardians now, there's no official reason for us to go down those steps, ride on the trains under the river, into the main city. Why would we want to go from here to there? We would be up to no good and they would know it.

The church is a small one, one of the first erected here, hundreds of years ago. It isn't used any more, except as a museum. Inside it you can see paintings, of women in long sombre dresses, their hair covered by white caps, and of upright men, darkly clothed and unsmiling. Our ancestors. Admission is free.

We don't go in, though, but stand on the path, looking at the churchyard. The old gravestones are still there, weathered, eroding, with their skulls and crossed bones, *memento mori*, their dough-faced angels, their winged hourglasses to remind us of the passing of mortal time, and, from a later century, their urns and willow trees, for mourning.

They haven't fiddled with the gravestones, or the church either. It's only the more recent history that offends them.

Ofglen's head is bowed, as if she's praying. She does this every time. Maybe, I think, there's someone, someone in particular gone, for her too; a man, a child. But I can't entirely believe it. I think of her as a woman for whom every act is done for show, is acting rather than a real act. She does such things to look good, I think. She's out to make the best of it.

But that is what I must look like to her, as well. How can it be otherwise?

Now we turn our backs on the church and there is the thing we've in truth come to see: the Wall.

The Wall is hundreds of years old too; or over a hundred, at least. Like the sidewalks, it's red brick, and must once have been plain but handsome. Now the gates have sentries and there are ugly new floodlights mounted on metal posts above it, and barbed wire along the bottom and broken glass set in concrete along the top.

No one goes through those gates willingly. The precautions are for those trying to get out, though to make it even as far as the Wall, from the inside, past the electronic alarm system, would be next to impossible.

Beside the main gateway there are six more bodies hanging, by the necks, their hands tied in front of them, their heads in white bags tipped sideways onto their shoulders. There must have been a Men's Salvaging early this morning. I didn't hear the bells. Perhaps I've become used to them.

We stop, together as if on signal, and stand and look at the bodies. It doesn't matter if we look. We're supposed to look: this is what they are there for, hanging on the Wall. Sometimes they'll be there for days, until there's a new batch, so as many people as possible will have the chance to see them.

What they are hanging from is hooks. The hooks have been set into the brickwork of the Wall, for this purpose. Not all of them are occupied. The hooks look like appliances for the armless. Or steel question marks, upside-down and sideways.

It's the bags over the heads that are the worst, worse than the faces themselves would be. It makes the men look like dolls on which faces have not yet been painted; like scarecrows, which in a way is what they are, since they are meant to scare. Or as if their heads are sacks, stuffed with some undifferentiated material, like flour or dough. It's the obvious heaviness of the heads, their vacancy, the way gravity pulls them down and there's no life any more to hold them up. The heads are Zeros.

Though if you look and look, as we are doing, you can see the outlines of the features under the white cloth, like grey shadows. The heads are the heads of snowmen, with the coal eyes and the carrot noses fallen out. The heads are melting.

But on one bag there's blood, which has seeped through the white cloth, where the mouth must have been. It makes another mouth, a small red one, like the mouths painted with thick brushes by kindergarten children. A child's idea of a smile. This smile of blood is what fixes the attention, finally. These are not snowmen after all.

The men wear white coats, like those worn by doctors or scientists. Doctors and scientists aren't the only ones, there are others, but they must have had a run on them this morning. Each has a placard hung around his neck to show why he has been executed: a drawing of a human foetus. They were doctors, then, in the time before, when such things were legal. Angel makers, they used to call them: or was that something else? They've been turned up now by the searches through hospital records, or – more likely, since most hospitals destroyed such records once it became clear what was going to happen – by informants: ex-nurses perhaps, or a pair of them, since evidence from a single woman is no longer admissible; or another doctor, hoping to save his own skin; or someone already accused, lashing out at an enemy, or at random, in some desperate bid for safety. Though informants are not always pardoned.

These men, we've been told, are like war criminals. It's no excuse that what they did was legal at the time: their crimes are retroactive. They have committed atrocities, and must be made into examples, for the rest. Though this is hardly needed. No woman in her right mind, these days, would seek to prevent a birth, should she be so lucky as to conceive.

What we are supposed to feel towards these bodies is hatred and scorn. This isn't what I feel. These bodies hanging on the Wall are time travellers, anachronisms. They've come here from the past.

What I feel towards them is blankness. What I feel is that I must not feel. What I feel is partly relief, because none of these men is Luke. Luke wasn't a doctor. Isn't.

I LOOK AT the one red smile. The red of the smile is the same as the red of the tulips in Serena Joy's garden, towards the base of the flowers where they are beginning to heal. The red is the same but there is no connection. The tulips are not tulips of blood, the red smiles are not flowers, neither thing makes a comment on the other. The tulips is not a reason for disbelief in the hanged man, or vice versa. Each thing is valid and really there. It is through a field of such valid objects that I must pick my way, every day and in every way. I put a lot of effort into making such distinctions. I need to make them. I need to be very clear, in my own mind.

I FEEL A tremor in the woman beside me. Is she crying? In what way could it make her look good? I can't afford to know. My own hands are clenched, I note, tight around the handle of my basket. I won't give anything away.

Ordinary, said Aunt Lydia, is what you are used to. This may not seem ordinary to you now, but after a time it will. It will become ordinary.

Three

THE NIGHT IS mine, my own time, to do with as I will, as long as I am quiet. As long as I don't move. As long as I lie still. The difference between *lie* and *lay*. Lay is always passive. Even men used to say, I'd like to get laid. Though sometimes they said, I'd like to lay her. All this is pure speculation. I don't really know what men used to say. I had only their words for it.

I lie, then, inside the room, under the plaster eye in the ceiling, behind the white curtains, between the sheets, neatly as they, and step sideways out of my own time. Out of time. Though this is time, nor am I out of it.

But the night is my time out. Where should I go?

SOMEWHERE GOOD.

Moira, sitting on the edge of my bed, legs crossed, ankle on knee, in her purple overalls, one dangly earring, the gold fingernail she wore to be eccentric, a cigarette between her stubby yellow-ended fingers. Let's go for a beer.

You're getting ashes in my bed, I said.

If you'd make it you wouldn't have this problem, said Moira.

In half an hour, I said. I had a paper due the next day. What was it? Psychology, English, Economics. We studied things like that, then. On the floor of the room there were books, open face down, this way and that, extravagantly.

Now, said Moira. You don't need to paint your face, it's only me. What's your paper on? I just did one on date rape.

Date rape, I said. You're so trendy. It sounds like some kind of dessert. *Date Rapé.*

Ha ha, said Moira. Get your coat.

She got it herself and tossed it at me. I'm borrowing five bucks off you, okay?

OR IN A park somewhere, with my mother. How old was I? It was cold, our breaths came out in front of us, there were no leaves on the trees; grey sky, two ducks in the pond, disconsolate. Breadcrumbs under my fingers, in my pocket. That's it: she said we were going to feed the ducks.

But there were some women burning books, that's what she was really there for. To see her friends; she'd lied to me, Saturdays were supposed to be my day. I turned away from her, sulking, towards the ducks, but the fire drew me back.

There were some men, too, among the women, and the books were magazines. They must have poured gasoline, because the flames shot high, and then they began dumping the magazines, from boxes, not too many at a time. Some of them were chanting; onlookers gathered.

Their faces were happy, ecstatic almost. Fire can do that. Even my mother's face, usually pale, thinnish, looked ruddy and cheerful, like a Christmas card; and there was another woman, large, with a soot smear down her cheek and an orange knitted cap, I remember her.

You want to throw one on, honey? she said. How old was I?

Good riddance to bad rubbish, she said, chuckling. It okay? she said to my mother.

If she wants to, my mother said; she had a way of talking about me to others as if I couldn't hear.

The woman handed me one of the magazines. It had a pretty woman on it, with no clothes on, hanging from the ceiling by a chain wound around her hands. I looked at it with interest. It didn't frighten me. I thought she was swinging, like Tarzan from a vine, on the TV.

Don't let her *see* it, said my mother. Here, she said to me, toss it in, quick.

I threw the magazine into the flames. It riffled open in the wind of its burning; big flakes of paper came loose, sailed into the air, still on fire, parts of women's bodies, turning to black ash in the air, before my eyes.

BUT THEN WHAT happens, but then what happens?

I know I lost time.

There must have been needles, pills, something like that. I couldn't have lost that much time without help. You have had a shock, they said.

I would come up through a roaring and confusion, like surf boiling. I can remember feeling quite calm. I can remember screaming, it felt like screaming though it may have been only a whisper, *Where is she? What have you done with her?*

There was no night or day; only a flickering. After a while there were chairs again, and a bed, and after that a window.

She's in good hands, they said. With people who are fit. You are unfit, but you want the best for her. Don't you?

They showed me a picture of her, standing outside on a lawn, her face a closed oval. Her light hair was pulled back tight behind her head. Holding her hand was a woman I didn't know. She was only as tall as the woman's elbow.

You've killed her, I said. She looked like an angel, solemn, compact, made of air.

She was wearing a dress I'd never seen, white and down to the ground.

I WOULD LIKE to believe this is a story I'm telling. I need to believe it. I must believe it. Those who can believe that such stories are only stories have a better chance.

If it's a story I'm telling, then I have control over the ending. Then there will be an ending, to the story, and real life will come after it. I can pick up where I left off.

It isn't a story I'm telling.

It's also a story I'm telling, in my head, as I go along.

Tell, rather than write, because I have nothing to write with and writing is in any case forbidden. But if it's a story, even in my head, I must be telling it to someone. You don't tell a story only to yourself. There's always someone else.

Even when there is no one.

A story is like a letter. *Dear You*, I'll say. Just you, without a name. Attaching a name attaches *you* to the world of fact, which is riskier, more hazardous: who knows what the chances are out there, of survival, yours? I will say *you*, *you*, like an old love song. *You* can mean more than one.

You can mean thousands.

I'm not in any immediate danger, I'll say to you.

I'll pretend you can hear me.

But it's no good, because I know you can't.

Four

THE GOOD WEATHER holds. It's almost like June, when we would get out our sundresses and our sandals and go for an ice-cream cone. There are three new bodies on the Wall. One is a priest, still wearing the black cassock. That's been put on him, for the trial, even though they gave up wearing those years ago, when the sect wars first began; cassocks made them too conspicuous. The two others have purple placards hung around their necks: Gender Treachery. Their bodies still wear the Guardian uniforms. Caught together, they must have been, but where? A barracks, a shower? It's hard to say. The snowman with the red smile is gone.

'We should go back,' I say to Ofglen. I'm always the one to say this. Sometimes I feel that if I didn't say it, she would stay here forever. But is she mourning or gloating? I still can't tell.

Without a word she swivels, as if she's voice-activated, as if she's on little oiled wheels, as if she's on top of a music box. I resent this grace of hers. I resent her meek head, bowed as if into a heavy wind. But there is no wind.

We leave the Wall, walk back the way we came, in the warm sun.

'It's a beautiful May day,' Ofglen says. I feel rather than see her head turn towards me, waiting for a reply.

'Yes,' I say. 'Praise be,' I add as an afterthought. *Mayday* used to be a distress signal, a long time ago, in one of those wars we studied in high school. I kept getting them mixed up, but you could tell them apart by the airplanes if you paid attention. It was Luke who told me about Mayday though. *Mayday, Mayday,* for pilots whose planes had been hit, and ships – was it ships too? – at sea. Maybe it was SOS for ships. I wish I could look it up. And it was something from Beethoven, for the beginning of the victory, in one of those wars.

Do you know what it came from? said Luke. Mayday?

No, I said. It's a strange word to use for that, isn't it?

Newspapers and coffee, on Sunday mornings, before she was born. There were still newspapers, then. We used to read them in bed.

It's French, he said. From *M'aidez.*

Help me.

COMING TOWARDS US there's a small procession, a funeral: three women, each with a black transparent veil thrown over her headdress. An Econowife and two others, the mourners, also Econowives, her friends perhaps. Their striped dresses are worn-looking, as are their faces. Some day, when times improve, says Aunt Lydia, no one will have to be an Econowife.

The first one is the bereaved, the mother; she carries a small black jar. From the size of the jar you can tell how old it was when it foundered, inside her, flowed to its death. Two or three months, too young to tell whether or not it was an Unbaby. The older ones and those that die at birth have boxes.

We pause, out of respect, while they go by. I wonder if Ofglen feels what I do, a pain like a stab, in the belly. We put our hands over our hearts to show these stranger women that we feel with them in their loss. Beneath her veil the first one scowls at us. One of the others turns aside, spits on the sidewalk. The Econowives do not like us.

WE GO PAST the shops and come to the barrier again, and are passed through. We continue on among the large empty-looking houses, the weedless lawns. At the corner near the house where I'm posted, Ofglen stops, turns to me.

'Under His Eye,' she says. The right farewell.

'Under His Eye,' I reply, and she gives a little nod. She hesitates, as if to say something more, but then she turns away and walks down the street. I watch her. She's like my own reflection, in a mirror from which I am moving away.

In the driveway, Nick is polishing the Whirlwind again. He's reached the chrome at the back. I put my gloved hand on the latch of the gate, open it, push inward. The gate clicks behind me. The tulips along the border are redder than ever, opening, no longer winecups but chalices; thrusting themselves up, to what end? They are, after all, empty. When they are old they turn themselves inside out, then explode slowly, the petals thrown out like shards.

Nick looks up and begins to whistle. Then he says, 'Nice walk?'

I nod, but do not answer with my voice. He isn't supposed to speak to me. Of course some of them will try, said Aunt Lydia. All flesh is weak. All flesh is grass, I corrected her in my head. They can't help it, she said, God made them that way but He did not make you that way. He made you different. It's up to you to set the boundaries. Later you will be thanked.

In the garden behind the house the Commander's Wife is sitting, in the chair she's had brought out. Serena Joy, what a stupid name. It's like something you'd put on your hair, in the other time, the time before, to straighten it. *Serena Joy*, it would say on the bottle, with a woman's head in cut-paper silhouette on a pink oval background with scalloped gold edges. With everything to choose from in the way of names, why did she pick that one? Serena Joy was never her real name, not even then. Her real name was Pam. I read that in a profile on her, in a news magazine, long after I'd first watched her singing while my mother slept in on Sunday mornings. By that time she was worthy of a profile: *Time* or *Newsweek* it was, it must have been. She wasn't singing any more by then, she was making speeches. She was good at it. Her speeches were about the sanctity of the home, about how women should stay home. Serena Joy didn't do this herself, she made speeches instead, but she presented this failure of hers as a sacrifice she was making for the good of all.

Around that time, someone tried to shoot her and missed; her secretary, who was standing right behind her, was killed instead. Someone else planted a bomb in her car but it went off too early. Though some people said she'd put the bomb in her own car, for sympathy. That's how hot things were getting.

Luke and I would watch her sometimes on the late-night news. Bathrobes, nightcaps. We'd watch her sprayed hair and her hysteria, and the tears she could still produce at will, and the mascara blackening her cheeks. By that time she was wearing more makeup. We thought she was funny. Or Luke thought she was funny. I only pretended to think so. Really she was a little frightening. She was in earnest.

She doesn't make speeches any more. She has become speechless. She stays in her home, but it doesn't seem to agree with her. How furious she must be, now that she's been taken at her word.

She's looking at the tulips. Her cane is beside her, on

the grass. Her profile is towards me, I can see that in the quick sideways look I take at her as I go past. It wouldn't do to stare. It's no longer a flawless cut-paper profile, her face is sinking in upon itself, and I think of those towns built on underground rivers, where houses and whole streets disappear overnight, into sudden quagmires, or coal towns collapsing into the mines beneath them. Something like this must have happened to her, once she saw the true shape of things to come.

She doesn't turn her head. She doesn't acknowledge my presence in any way, although she knows I'm there. I can tell she knows, it's like a smell, her knowledge; something gone sour, like old milk.

It's not the husbands you have to watch out for, said Aunt Lydia, it's the Wives. You should always try to imagine what they must be feeling. Of course they will resent you. It is only natural. Try to feel for them. Aunt Lydia thought she was very good at feeling for other people. Try to pity them. Forgive them, for they know not what they do. Again the tremulous smile, of a beggar, the weak-eyed blinking, the gaze upwards, through the round steel-rimmed glasses, towards the back of the classroom, as if the green-painted plaster ceiling were opening and God on a cloud of Pink Pearl face powder were coming down through the wires and sprinkler plumbing. You must realize that they are defeated women. They have been unable . . .

Here her voice broke off, and there was a pause, during which I could hear a sigh, a collective sigh from those around me. It was a bad idea to rustle or fidget during these pauses: Aunt Lydia might look abstracted but she was aware of every twitch. So there was only the sigh.

The future is in your hands, she resumed. She held her own hands out to us, the ancient gesture that was both an offering and an invitation, to come forward, into an embrace, an acceptance. In your hands, she said, looking down at her own hands as if they had given her the idea. But there was nothing in them. They were empty. It was our hands that were supposed to be full, of the future; which could be held but not seen.

I WALK AROUND to the back door, open it, go in, set my basket down on the kitchen table. The table has been scrubbed off, cleared of flour; today's bread, freshly baked, is cooling on its rack. The kitchen smells of yeast, a nostalgic smell. It reminds me of other kitchens, kitchens that were mine. It smells of mothers; although my own mother did not make bread. It smells of me, in former times, when I was a mother.

This is a treacherous smell, and I know I must shut it out.

Rita is there, sitting at the table, peeling and slicing carrots. Old carrots they are, thick ones, over-wintered, bearded from their time in storage. The new carrots, tender and pale, won't be ready for weeks. The knife she uses is sharp and bright, and tempting. I would like to have a knife like that.

Rita stops chopping the carrots, stands up, takes the parcels out of the basket, almost eagerly. She looks forward to seeing what I've brought, although she always frowns while opening the parcels; nothing I bring fully pleases her. She's thinking she could have done better herself. She would rather do the shopping, get exactly what she wants; she envies me the walk. In this house we all envy each other something.

'They've got oranges,' I say. 'At Milk and Honey. There are still some left.' I hold out this idea to her like an offering. I wish to ingratiate myself. I saw the oranges yesterday, but I didn't tell Rita; yesterday she was too grumpy. 'I could get some, tomorrow, if you'd give me the tokens for them.' I hold out the chicken to her. She wanted steak today, but there wasn't any.

Rita grunts, not revealing pleasure or acceptance. She'll think about it, the grunt says, in her own sweet time. She undoes the string on the chicken, and the glazed paper. She prods the chicken, flexes a wing, pokes a finger into the cavity, fishes out the giblets. The chicken lies there, headless and without feet, goose-pimpled as though shivering.

'Bath day,' Rita says, without looking at me.

Cora comes into the kitchen, from the pantry at the back, where they keep the mops and brooms. 'A chicken,' she says, almost with delight.

'Scrawny,' says Rita, 'but it'll have to do.'

'There wasn't much else,' I say. Rita ignores me.

'Looks big enough to me,' says Cora. Is she standing up for me? I look at her, to see if I should smile; but no, it's only the food she's thinking of. She's younger than Rita; the sunlight, coming slant now through the west window, catches her hair, parted and drawn back. She must have been pretty, quite recently. There's a little mark, like a dimple, in each of her ears, where the punctures for earrings have grown over.

'Tall,' says Rita, 'but bony. You should speak up,' she says to me, looking directly at me for the first time. 'Ain't like you're common.' She means the Commander's rank. But in the other sense, her sense, she thinks I am common. She is over sixty, her mind's made up.

She goes to the sink, runs her hands briefly under the tap, dries them on the dishtowel. The dishtowel is white with blue stripes. Dishtowels are the same as they always were. Sometimes these flashes of normality come at me from the side, like ambushes. The ordinary, the usual, a reminder, like a kick. I see the dishtowel, out of context, and I catch my breath. For some, in some ways, things haven't changed that much.

'Who's doing the bath?' says Rita, to Cora, not to me. 'I got to tenderize this bird.'

'I'll do it later,' says Cora, 'after the dusting.'

'Just so it gets done,' says Rita.

They're talking about me as though I can't hear. To them I'm a household chore, one among many.

I've been dismissed. I pick up the basket, go through the kitchen door and along the hall towards the grandfather clock. The sitting-room door is closed. Sun comes through the fanlight, falling in colours across the floor: red and blue, purple. I step into it briefly, stretch out my hands; they fill with flowers of light. I go up the stairs, my face, distant and white and distorted, framed in the hall mirror, which bulges outward like an eye under pressure. I follow the dusty-pink runner down the long upstairs hallway, back to the room.

There's someone standing in the hall, near the door to the room where I stay. The hall is dusky, this is a man, his back to me; he's looking into the room, dark against its light. I can see now, it's the Commander, he isn't supposed to be here. He hears me coming, turns, hesitates, walks forward. Towards me. He is violating custom, what do I do now?

I stop, he pauses, I can't see his face, he's looking at me, what does he want? But then he moves forward again, steps to the side to avoid touching me, inclines his head, is gone.

Something has been shown to me, but what is it? Like the flag of an unknown country, seen for an instant above a curve of hill, it could mean attack, it could mean parley, it could mean the edge of something, a territory. The signals animals give one another: lowered blue eyelids, ears laid back, raised hackles. A flash of bared teeth, what in hell does he think he's doing? Nobody else has seen him. I hope. Was he invading? Was he in my room?

I called it *mine*.

Five

MY ROOM, THEN. There has to be some space, finally, that I claim as mine, even in this time.

I'm waiting, in my room, which right now is a waiting room. When I go to bed it's a bedroom. The curtains are still wavering in the small wind, the sun outside is still shining, though not in through the window directly. It has moved west. I am trying not to tell stories, or at any rate not this one.

SOMEONE HAS LIVED in this room, before me. Someone like me, or I prefer to believe so.

I discovered it three days after I was moved here.

I had a lot of time to pass. I decided to explore the room. Not hastily, as one would explore a hotel room, expecting no surprise, opening and shutting the desk drawers, the cupboard doors, unwrapping the tiny individually wrapped bar of soap, prodding the pillows. Will I ever be in a hotel room again? How I wasted them, those rooms, that freedom from being seen.

Rented licence.

In the afternoons, when Luke was still in flight from his wife, when I was still imaginary for him. Before we were married and I solidified. I would always get there first, check in. It wasn't that many times, but it seems now like a decade, an era; I can remember what I wore, each blouse, each scarf. I would pace, waiting for him, turn the television on and then off, dab behind my ears with perfume, Opium it was. It came in a Chinese bottle, red and gold.

I was nervous. How was I to know he loved me? It might be just an affair. Why did we ever say *just*? Though at that time men and women tried each other on, casually, like suits, rejecting whatever did not fit.

The knock would come at the door; I'd open, with relief, desire. He was so momentary, so condensed. And yet there seemed no end to him. We would lie in those afternoon beds, afterwards, hands on each other, talking it over. Possible, impossible. What could be done? We thought we had such problems. How were we to know we were happy?

But now it's the rooms themselves I miss as well, even the dreadful paintings that hung on the walls, landscapes with fall foliage or snow melting in hardwoods, or women in period costume, with china-doll faces and bustles and parasols, or sad-eyed clowns, or bowls of fruit, stiff and chalky-looking. The fresh towels ready for spoilage, the wastebaskets gaping their invitations, beckoning in the careless junk. Careless. I was careless, in those rooms. I could lift the telephone and food would appear on a tray, food I had chosen. Food that was bad for me, no doubt, and drink too. There were Bibles in the dresser drawers, put there by some charitable society, though probably no one read them very much. There were post-cards, too, with pictures of the hotel on them, and you could write on the postcards and send them to anyone you wanted. It seems like such an impossible thing, now; like something you'd make up.

So. I explored this room, not hastily, then, like a hotel room, wasting it. I didn't want to do it all at once, I wanted to make it last. I divided the room into sections, in my head; I allowed myself one section a day. This one section I would examine with the greatest minuteness: the un-evenness of the plaster under the wallpaper, the scratches in the paint of the baseboard and the windowsill, under the top coat of paint, the stains on the mattress, for I went so far as to lift the blankets and sheets from the bed, fold them back, a little at a time, so they could be replaced quickly if anyone came.

The stains on the mattress. Like dried flower petals. Not recent. Old love; there's no other kind of love in this room now.

When I saw that, that evidence left by two people, of

love or something like it, desire at least, at least touch, between two people now perhaps old or dead, I covered the bed again and lay down on it. I looked up at the blind plaster eye in the ceiling. I wanted to feel Luke lying beside me. I have them, these attacks of the past, like faintness, a wave sweeping over my head. Sometimes it can hardly be borne. What is to be done, what is to be done, I thought. There is nothing to be done. They also serve who only stand and wait. Or lie down and wait. I know why the glass in the window is shatterproof, and why they took down the chandelier. I wanted to feel Luke lying beside me, but there wasn't room.

I SAVED THE cupboard until the third day. I looked carefully over the door first, inside and out, then the walls with their brass hooks – how could they have overlooked the hooks? Why didn't they remove them? Too close to the floor? But still, a stocking, that's all you'd need. And the rod with the plastic hangers, my dresses hanging on them, the red woollen cape for cold weather, the shawl. I knelt to examine the floor, and there it was, in tiny writing, quite fresh it seemed, scratched with a pin or maybe just a fingernail, in the corner where the darkest shadow fell: *Nolite te bastardes carborundorum.*

I didn't know what it meant, or even what language it was in. I thought it might be Latin, but I didn't know any Latin. Still, it was a message, and it was in writing, forbidden by that very fact, and it hadn't yet been discovered.

Except by me, for whom it was intended. It was intended for whoever came next.

It pleases me to ponder this message. It pleases me to think I'm communing with her, this unknown woman. For she is unknown; or if known, she has never been mentioned to me. It pleases me to know that her taboo message made it through, to at least one other person, washed itself up on the wall of my cupboard, was opened and read by me. Sometimes I repeat the words to myself. They give me a small joy. When I imagine the woman who wrote them, I think of her as about my age, maybe a little younger. I turn her into Moira, Moira as she was when she was in college, in the room next to mine: quirky, jaunty, athletic, with a bicycle once, and a knapsack for hiking. Freckles, I think; irreverent, resourceful.

I wonder who she was or is, and what's become of her.

I tried that out on Rita, the day I found the message.

Who was the woman who stayed in that room? I said. Before me? If I'd asked it differently, if I'd said, Was there a woman who stayed in that room before me? I might not have got anywhere.

Which one? she said; she sounded grudging, suspicious, but then, she almost always sounds like that when she speaks to me.

So there have been more than one. Some haven't stayed their full term of posting, their full two years. Some have been sent away, for one reason or another. Or maybe not sent; gone?

The lively one. I was guessing. The one with freckles.

You knew her? Rita asked, more suspicious than ever.

I knew her before, I lied. I heard she was here.

Rita accepted this. She knows there must be a grapevine, an underground of sorts.

She didn't work out, she said.

In what way? I asked, trying to sound as neutral as possible.

But Rita clamped her lips together. I am like a child here, there are some things I must not be told. What you don't know won't hurt you, was all she would say.

Six

SOMETIMES I SING to myself, in my head; something lugubrious, mournful, presbyterian:

Amazing grace, how sweet the sound
Could save a wretch like me,
Who once was lost, but now am found,
Was bound, but now am free.

I don't know if the words are right. I can't remember. Such songs are not sung any more in public, especially the ones that use words like *free*. They are considered too dangerous. They belong to outlawed sects.

I feel so lonely, baby,
I feel so lonely, baby,
I feel so lonely I could die.

This too is outlawed. I know it from an old cassette tape, of my mother's; she had a scratchy and untrust-worthy machine, too, that could still play such things. She used to put the tape on when her friends came over and they'd had a few drinks.

I don't sing like this often. It makes my throat hurt.

There isn't much music in this house, except what we hear on the TV. Sometimes Rita will hum, while kneading or peeling; a wordless humming, tuneless, unfathomable. And sometimes from the front sitting room there will be the thin sound of Serena's voice, from a disc made long ago and played now with the volume low, so she won't be caught listening as she sits there knitting, remembering her own former and now amputated glory: *Hallelujah*.

It's warm for this time of year. Houses like this heat up in the sun, there's not enough insulation. Around me the air is stagnant, despite the little current, the breath coming in past the curtains. I'd like to be able to open the window as wide as it could go. Soon we'll be allowed to change into the summer dresses.

The summer dresses are unpacked and hanging in the closet, two of them, pure cotton, which is better than synthetics like the cheaper ones, though even so, when it's muggy, in July and August, you sweat inside them. No worry about sunburn though, said Aunt Lydia. The spectacles women used to make of themselves. Oiling themselves like roast meat on a spit, and bare backs and shoulders, on the street, in public, and legs, not even stockings on them, no wonder those things used to happen. *Things*, the word she used when whatever it stood for was too distasteful or filthy or horrible to pass her lips. A successful life for her was one that avoided *things*, excluded *things*. Such *things* do not happen to nice women. And not good for the complexion, not at all, wrinkle you up like a dried apple. But we weren't supposed to care about our complexions any more, she'd forgotten that.

In the park, said Aunt Lydia, lying on blankets, men and women together sometimes, and at that she began to cry, standing up there in front of us, in full view.

I'm doing my best, she said. I'm trying to give you the best chance you can have. She blinked, the light was too strong for her, her mouth trembled, around her front teeth, teeth that stuck out a little and were long and yellowish, and I thought about the dead mice we would find on our doorstep, when we lived in a house, all three of us, four counting our cat, who was the one making these offerings.

Aunt Lydia pressed her hand over her mouth of a dead rodent. After a minute she took her hand away. I wanted to cry too because she reminded me. If only she wouldn't eat half of them first, I said to Luke.

Don't think it's easy for me either, said Aunt Lydia.

MOIRA, BREEZING INTO my room, dropping her denim jacket on the floor. Got any cigs, she said.

In my purse, I said. No matches though.

Moira rummages in my purse. You should throw out some of this junk, she says. I'm giving an underwhore party.

A what? I say. There's no point trying to work, Moira won't allow it, she's like a cat that crawls onto the page when you're trying to read.

You know, like Tupperware, only with underwear. Tarts' stuff. Lace crotches, snap garters. Bras that push your tits up. She finds my lighter, lights the cigarette she's extracted from my purse. Want one? Tosses the package, with great generosity considering they're mine.

Thanks piles, I say sourly. You're crazy. Where'd you get an idea like that?

Working my way through college, says Moira. I've got connections. Friend of my mother's. It's big in the suburbs, once they start getting age spots they figure they've got to beat the competition. The Pornomarts and what have you.

I'm laughing. She always made me laugh.

But here? I say. Who'll come? Who needs it?

You're never too young to learn, she says. Come on, it'll be great. We'll all pee our pants laughing.

IS THAT HOW we lived then? But we lived as usual. Everyone does, most of the time. Whatever is going on is as usual. Even this is as usual, now.

We lived, as usual, by ignoring. Ignoring isn't the same as ignorance, you have to work at it.

Nothing changes instantaneously: in a gradually heating bathtub you'd be boiled to death before you knew it. There were stories in the newspapers, of course, corpses in ditches or the woods, bludgeoned to death or mutilated, interfered with as they used to say, but they were about other women, and the men who did such things were other men. None of them were the men we knew. The newspaper stories were like dreams to us, bad dreams dreamt by others. How awful, we would say, and they were, but they were awful without being believable. They were too melodramatic, they had a dimension that was not the dimension of our lives.

We were the people who were not in the papers. We lived in the blank white spaces at the edges of print. It gave us more freedom.

We lived in the gaps between the stories.

FROM BELOW, FROM the driveway, comes the sound of the car being started. It's quiet in this area, there isn't a lot of traffic, you can hear things like that very clearly: car motors, lawn mowers, the clipping of a hedge, the slam of a door. You could hear a shout clearly, or a shot, if such noises were ever made here. Sometimes there are distant sirens.

I go to the window and sit on the window seat, which is too narrow for comfort. There's a hard little cushion on it, with a petit-point cover: FAITH, in square print, surrounded by a wreath of lilies. FAITH is a faded blue, the leaves of the lilies a dingy green. This is a cushion once used elsewhere, worn but not enough to throw out. Somehow it's been overlooked.

We lived in the blank white spaces at the edges of print. It gave us more freedom

I can spend minutes, tens of minutes, running my eyes over the print: FAITH. It's the only thing they've given me to read. If I were caught doing it, would it count? I didn't put the cushion here myself.

The motor turns, and I lean forward, pulling the white curtain across my face, like a veil. It's semi-sheer, I can see through it. If I press my forehead against the glass and look down, I can see the back half of the Whirlwind. Nobody is there, but as I watch I see Nick come around to the back door of the car, open it, stand stiffly beside it. His cap is straight now and his sleeves rolled down and buttoned. I can't see his face because I'm looking down on him.

Now the Commander is coming out. I glimpse him only for an instant, foreshortened, walking to the car. He doesn't have his hat on, so it's not a formal event he's going to. His hair is grey. Silver, you might call it if you were being kind. I don't feel like being kind. The one before this was bald, so I suppose he's an improvement.

If I could spit, out the window, or throw something, the cushion for instance, I might be able to hit him.

MOIRA AND I, with paper bags filled with water. Water bombs, they were called. Leaning out my dorm window, dropping them on the heads of the boys below. It was Moira's idea. What were they trying to do? Climb a ladder, for something. For our underwear.

That dormitory had once been co-educational, there

were still urinals in one of the washrooms on our floor. But by the time I'd got there they'd put the men and women back the way they were.

The Commander stoops, gets into the car, disappears, and Nick shuts the door. A moment later the car moves backwards, down the driveway and onto the street, and vanishes behind the hedge.

I ought to feel hatred for this man. I know I ought to feel it, but it isn't what I do feel. What I feel is more complicated than that. I don't know what to call it. It isn't love.

Seven

YESTERDAY MORNING I went to the doctor. Was taken, by a Guardian, one of those with the red armbands who are in charge of such things. We rode in a red car, him in the front, me in the back. No twin went with me; on these occasions I'm solitaire.

I'm taken to the doctor's once a month, for tests: urine, hormones, cancer smear, blood test; the same as before, except that now it's obligatory.

The doctor's office is in a modern office building. We ride up in the elevator, silently, the Guardian facing me. In the black mirror wall of the elevator I can see the back of his head. At the office itself, I go in; he waits, outside in the hall, with the other Guardians, on one of the chairs placed there for that purpose.

Inside the waiting room there are other women, three of them, in red: this doctor is a specialist. Covertly we regard each other, sizing up each other's bellies: is anyone lucky? The nurse records our names and the numbers from our passes on the Compudoc, to see if we are who we are supposed to be. He's six feet tall, about forty, a diagonal scar across his cheek; he sits typing, his hands too big for the keyboard, still wearing his pistol in the shoulder holster.

When I'm called I go through the doorway into the inner room. It's white, featureless, like the outer one, except for a folding screen, red cloth stretched on a frame, a gold eye painted on it, with a snake-twined sword upright beneath it, like a sort of handle. The snakes and the sword are bits of broken symbolism left over from the time before.

After I've filled the small bottle left ready for me in the little washroom, I take off my clothes, behind the screen, and leave them folded on the chair. When I'm naked I lie down on the examining table, on the sheet of chilly crackling disposable paper. I pull the second sheet, the cloth one, up over my body. At neck level there's another sheet, suspended from the ceiling. It intersects me so that the doctor will never see my face. He deals with a torso only.

When I'm arranged I reach my hand out, fumble for the small lever at the right side of the table, pull it back. Somewhere else a bell rings, unheard by me. After a minute the door opens, footsteps come in, there is breathing. He isn't supposed to speak to me except when it's absolutely necessary. But this doctor is talkative.

'How are we getting along?' he says, some tic of speech from the other time. The sheet is lifted from my skin, a draft pimples me. A cold finger, rubber-clad and jellied, slides into me, I am poked and prodded. The finger retreats, enters otherwise, withdraws.

'Nothing wrong with you,' the doctor says, as if to himself. 'Any pain, honey?' He calls me *honey*.

'No,' I say.

My breasts are fingered in their turn, a search for ripeness, rot. The breathing comes nearer, I smell old smoke, aftershave, tobacco dust on hair. Then the voice, very soft, close to my head: that's him, bulging the sheet.

'I could help you,' he says. Whispers.

'What?' I say.

'Shh,' he says. 'I could help you. I've helped others.'

'Help me?' I say, my voice as low as his. 'How?' Does he know something, has he seen Luke, has he found, can he bring back?

'How do you think?' he says, still barely breathing it. Is that his hand, sliding up my leg? He's taken off the glove. 'The door's locked. No one will come in. They'll never know it isn't his.'

He lifts the sheet. The lower part of his face is covered by the white gauze mask, regulation. Two brown eyes, a nose, a head with brown hair on it. His hand is between my legs. 'Most of those old guys can't make it any more,' he says. 'Or they're sterile.'

I almost gasp: he's said a forbidden word. *Sterile*. There

is no such thing as a sterile man any more, not officially. There are only women who are fruitful and women who are barren, that's the law.

'Lots of women do it,' he goes on. 'You want a baby, don't you?'

'Yes,' I say. It's true, and I don't ask why, because I know. *Give me children, or else I die.* There's more than one meaning to it.

'You're soft,' he says. 'It's time. Today or tomorrow would do it, why waste it? It'd only take a minute, honey.' What he called his wife, once; maybe still does, but really it's a generic term. We are all *honey.*

I hesitate. He's offering himself to me, his services, at some risk to himself.

'I hate to see what they put you through,' he murmurs. It's genuine, genuine sympathy; and yet he's enjoying this, sympathy and all. His eyes are moist with compassion, his hand is moving on me, nervously and with impatience.

'It's too dangerous,' I say. 'No. I can't.' The penalty is death. But they have to catch you in the act, with two witnesses. What are the odds, is the room bugged, who's waiting just outside the door?

His hand stops. 'Think about it,' he says. 'I've seen your chart. You don't have a lot of time left. But it's your life.'

'Thank you,' I say. I must leave the impression that I'm not offended, that I'm open to suggestion. He takes his hand away, lazily almost, lingeringly, this is not the last word as far as he's concerned. He could fake the tests, report me for cancer, for infertility, have me shipped off to the Colonies, with the Unwomen. None of this has been said, but the knowledge of his power hangs nevertheless in the air as he pats my thigh, withdraws himself behind the hanging sheet.

'Next month,' he says.

I put on my clothes again, behind the screen. My hands are shaking. Why am I frightened? I've crossed no boundaries, I've given no trust, taken no risk, all is safe. It's the choice that terrifies me. A way out, a salvation.

Eight

THE BATHROOM IS beside the bedroom. It's papered in small blue flowers, forget-me-nots, with curtains to match. There's a blue bathmat, a blue fake-fur cover on the toilet seat; all this bathroom lacks from the time before is a doll whose skirt conceals the extra roll of toilet paper. Except that the mirror over the sink has been taken out and replaced by an oblong of tin, and the door has no lock, and there are no razors, of course. There were incidents in bathrooms at first; there were cuttings, drownings. Before they got all the bugs ironed out. Cora sits on a chair outside in the hall, to see that no one else goes in. In a bathroom, in a bathtub, you are vulnerable, said Aunt Lydia. She didn't say to what.

The bath is a requirement, but it is also a luxury. Merely to lift off the heavy white wings and the veil, merely to feel my own hair again, with my hands, is a luxury. My hair is long now, untrimmed. Hair must be long but covered. Aunt Lydia said: Saint Paul said it's either that or a close shave. She laughed, that held-back neighing of hers, as if she'd told a joke.

Cora has run the bath. It steams like a bowl of soup. I take off the rest of my clothes, the overdress, the white shift and petticoat, the red stockings, the loose cotton pantaloons. Pantyhose gives you crotch rot, Moira used to say. Aunt Lydia would never have used an expression like *crotch rot. Unhygenic* was hers. She wanted everything to be very hygenic.

My nakedness is strange to me already. My body seems outdated. Did I really wear bathing suits, at the beach? I did, without thought, among men, without caring that my legs, my arms, my thighs and back were on display, could be seen. *Shameful, immodest.* I avoid looking down at my body, not so much because it's shameful or immodest but because I don't want to see it. I don't want to look at something that determines me so completely.

I STEP INTO the water, lie down, let it hold me. The water is soft as hands. I close my eyes, and she's there with me, suddenly, without warning, it must be the smell of the soap. I put my face against the soft hair at the back of her neck and breathe her in, baby powder and child's washed flesh and shampoo, with an undertone, the faint scent of urine. This is the age she is when I'm in the bath. She comes back to me at different ages. This is how I know she's not really a ghost. If she were a ghost she would be the same age always.

One day, when she was eleven months old, just before she began to walk, a woman stole her out of a supermarket cart. It was a Saturday, which was when Luke and I did the week's shopping, because both of us had jobs. She was sitting in the little baby seats they had then, in supermarket carts, with holes for the legs. She was happy enough, and I'd turned my back, the cat-food section I think it was; Luke was over at the side of the store, out of sight, at the meat counter. He liked to choose what kind of meat we were going to eat during the week. He said men needed more meat than women did, and that it wasn't a superstition and he wasn't being a jerk, studies had been done. There are some differences, he said. He was fond of saying that, as if I was trying to prove there weren't. But mostly he said it when my mother was there. He liked to tease her.

I heard her start to cry. I turned around and she was disappearing down the aisle, in the arms of a woman I'd never seen before. I screamed, and the woman was stopped. She must have been about thirty-five. She was crying and saying it was her baby, the Lord had given it to her, he'd sent her a sign. I felt sorry for her. The store manager apologized and they held her until the police came.

She's just crazy, Luke said.

I thought it was an isolated incident, at the time.

* * *

SHE FADES, I can't keep her here with me, she's gone now. Maybe I do think of her as a ghost, the ghost of a dead girl, a little girl who died when she was five. I remember the pictures of us I had once, me holding her, standard poses, mother and baby, locked in a frame, for safety. Behind my closed eyes I can see myself as I am now, sitting beside an open drawer, or a trunk, in the cellar, where the baby clothes are folded away, a lock of hair, cut when she was two, in an envelope, white blonde. It got darker later.

I don't have those things any more, the clothes and hair. I wonder what happened to all our things. Looted, dumped out, carried away. Confiscated.

I've learned to do without a lot of things. If you have a lot of things, said Aunt Lydia, you get too attached to this material world and you forget about spiritual values. You must cultivate poverty of spirit. Blessed are the meek. She didn't go on to say anything about inheriting the earth.

I lie, lapped by the water, beside an open drawer that does not exist, and think about a girl who did not die when she was five; who still does exist, I hope, though not for me. Do I exist for her? Am I a picture somewhere, in the dark at the back of her mind?

They must have told her I was dead. That's what they would think of doing. They would say it would be easier for her to adjust.

EIGHT, SHE MUST be now. I've filled in the time I lost, I know how much there's been. They were right, it's easier, to think of her as dead. I don't have to hope then, or make a wasted effort. Why bash your head, said Aunt Lydia, against a wall? Sometimes she had a graphic way of putting things.

'I AIN'T GOT all day,' says Cora's voice outside the door. It's true, she hasn't. She hasn't got all of anything. I must not deprive her of her time. I soap myself, use the scrub brush and the piece of pumice for sanding off dead skin. Such puritan aids are supplied. I wish to be totally clean, germless, without bacteria, like the surface of the moon. I will not be able to wash myself, this evening, not afterwards, not for a day. It interferes, they say, and why take chances?

I cannot avoid seeing, now, the small tattoo on my ankle. Four digits and an eye, a passport in reverse. It's supposed to guarantee that I will never be able to fade, finally, into another landscape. I am too important, too scarce, for that. I am a national resource.

I pull the plug, dry myself, put on my red terrycloth robe. I leave today's dress here, where Cora will pick it up to be washed. Back in the room I dress again. The white headdress isn't necessary for the evening, because I won't be going out. Everyone in this house knows what my face looks like. The red veil goes on, though, covering my damp hair, my head, which has not been shaved. Where did I see that film, about the women, kneeling in the town square, hands holding them, their hair falling in clumps?

I cannot avoid seeing, now, the small tattoo on my ankle. Four digits and an eye, a passport in reverse

What had they done? It must have been a long time ago, because I can't remember.

Cora brings my supper, covered, on a tray. She knocks at the door before entering. I like her for that. It means she thinks I have some of what we used to call privacy left.

'Thank you,' I say, taking the tray from her, and she actually smiles at me, but she turns away without answering. When we're alone together she's shy of me.

I put the tray on the small white-painted table and draw the chair up to it. I take the cover off the tray. The thigh of a chicken, overcooked. It's better than bloody, which is the other way she does it. Rita has ways of making her resentment felt. A baked potato, green beans, salad. Canned pears for desert. It's good enough food, though bland. Healthy food. You have to get your vitamins and minerals, said Aunt Lydia coyly. You must be a worthy vessel. No coffee or tea though, no alcohol. Studies have been done. There's a paper napkin, as in cafeterias.

I think of the others, those without. This is the heartland, here, I'm leading a pampered life, may the Lord make us truly grateful, said Aunt Lydia, or was it thankful, and I start to eat the food. I'm not hungry tonight. I feel sick to my stomach. But there's no place to put the food, no potted plants, and I won't chance the toilet. I'm too nervous, that's what it is. Could I leave it on the plate, ask Cora not to report me? I chew and swallow, chew and swallow, feeling the sweat come out. In my stomach the food balls itself together, a handful of damp cardboard, squeezed.

Downstairs, in the dining room, there will be candles on the large mahogany table, a white cloth, silver, flowers, wine glasses with wine in them. There will be a click of knives against china, a clink as she sets down her fork, with a barely audible sigh, leaving half the contents of her plate untouched. Possibly she will say she has no appetite. Possibly she won't say anything. If she says something, does he comment? If she doesn't say anything, does he notice? I wonder how she manages to get herself noticed. I think it must be hard.

THERE'S A PAT of butter on the side of the plate. I tear off a corner of the paper napkin, wrap the butter in it, take it to the cupboard and slip it into the toe of my right shoe, from the extra pair, as I have done before. I crumple up the rest of the napkin: no one, surely, will bother to smooth it out, to check if any is missing. I will use the butter later tonight. It would not do, this evening, to smell of butter.

I WAIT. I compose myself. My self is a thing I must now compose, as one composes a speech. What I must present is a made thing, not something born.

Nine

THERE'S TIME TO spare. This is one of the things I wasn't prepared for – the amount of unfilled time, the long parentheses of nothing. Time as white sound. If only I could embroider. Weave, knit, something to do with my hands. I want a cigarette. I remember walking in art galleries, through the nineteenth century: the obsession they had then with harems. Dozens of paintings of harems, fat women lolling on divans, turbans on their heads or velvet caps, being fanned with peacock tails, a eunuch in the background standing guard. Studies of sedentary flesh, painted by men who'd never been there. These pictures were supposed to be erotic, and I thought they were, at the time; but I see now what they were really about. They were paintings about suspended animation; about waiting, about objects not in use. They were paintings about boredom.

But maybe boredom is erotic, when women do it, for men.

I WAIT, WASHED, brushed, fed, like a prize pig. Sometime in the eighties they invented pig balls, for pigs who were being fattened in pens. Pig balls were large coloured balls; the pigs rolled them around with their snouts. The pig marketers said this improved their muscle tone; the pigs were curious, they liked to have something to think about.

I read about that in Introduction to Psychology; that, and the chapter on caged rats who'd give themselves electric shocks for something to do. And the one on the pigeons, trained to peck a button which made a grain of corn appear. Three groups of them: the first got one grain per peck, the second one grain every other peck, the third was random. When the man in charge cut off the grain, the first group gave up quite soon, the second group a little later. The third group never gave up. They'd peck themselves to death, rather than quit. Who knew what worked?

I wish I had a pig ball.

I LIE DOWN on the braided rug. You can always practise, said Aunt Lydia. Several sessions a day, fitted into your daily routine. Arms at the sides, knees bent, lift the pelvis, roll the backbone down. Tuck. Again. Breathe in to the count of five, hold, expel. We'd do that in what used to be the Domestic Science room, cleared now of sewing machines and washer-dryers; in unison, lying on little Japanese mats, a tape playing, *Les Sylphides*. That's what I hear now, in my head, as I lift, tilt, breathe. Behind my closed eyes thin white dancers flit gracefully among the trees, their legs fluttering like the wings of held birds.

IN THE AFTERNOONS we lay on our beds for an hour in the gymnasium, between three and four. They said it was a period of rest and meditation. I thought then they did it because they wanted some time off themselves, from teaching us, and I know the Aunts not on duty went off to the teachers' room for a cup of coffee, or whatever they called by that name. But now I think that the rest also was practice. They were giving us a chance to get used to blank time.

A catnap, Aunt Lydia called it, in her coy way.

The strange thing is we needed a rest. Many of us went to sleep. We were tired there, a lot of the time. We were on some kind of pill or drug I think, they put it in the food, to keep us calm. But maybe not. Maybe it was the place itself. After the first shock, after you'd come to terms, it was better to be lethargic. You could tell yourself you were saving up your strength.

I must have been there three weeks when Moira came. She was brought into the gymnasium by two of the Aunts, in the usual way, while we were having our nap. She still had her clothes on, jeans and a blue sweatshirt – her hair was short, she'd defied fashion as usual – so I recognized her at once. She saw me too, but she turned away, she already knew what was safe. There was a bruise on her left cheek, turning purple. The Aunts took her to a vacant bed where the red dress was already laid out. She undressed, began to dress again, in silence, the Aunts standing at the end of the bed, the rest of us watching from inside our slitted eyes. As she bent over I could see the knobs on her spine.

I couldn't talk to her for several days; we looked only, small glances, like sips. Friendships were suspicious, we knew it, we avoided each other during the mealtime line-ups in the cafeteria and in the halls between classes. But on the fourth day she was beside me during the walk, two by two around the football field. We weren't given the white wings until we graduated, we had only the veils; so we could talk, as long as we did it quietly and didn't turn to look at one another. The Aunts walked at the head of the line and at the end, so the only danger was from the others. Some were believers and might report us.

This is a loony bin, Moira said.

I'm so glad to see you, I said.

Where can we talk? said Moira.

Washroom, I said. Watch the clock. End stall, two-thirty.

That was all we said.

It makes me feel safer, that Moira is here. We can go to the washroom if we put our hands up, though there's a limit to how many times a day, they mark it down on a chart. I watch the clock, electric and round, at the front over the green blackboard. Two-thirty comes during Testifying. Aunt Helena is here, as well as Aunt Lydia, because Testifying is special. Aunt Helena is fat, she once headed a Weight Watchers' franchise operation in Iowa. She's good at Testifying.

It's Janine, telling about how she was gang-raped at fourteen and had an abortion. She told the same story last week. She seemed almost proud of it, while she was telling. It may not even be true. At Testifying, it's safer to make things up than to say you have nothing to reveal. But since it's Janine, it's probably more or less true.

But whose fault was it? Aunt Helena says, holding up one plump finger.

Her fault, *her* fault, *her* fault, we chant in unison.

Who led them on? Aunt Helena beams, pleased with us.

She did. *She* did. *She* did.

Why did God allow such a terrible thing to happen?

Teach her a *lesson*. Teach her a *lesson*. Teach her a *lesson*.

Last week, Janine burst into tears. Aunt Helena made her kneel at the front of the classroom, hands behind her back, where we could all see her, her red face and dripping nose. Her hair dull blonde, her eyelashes so light they seemed not there, the lost eyelashes of someone who's been in a fire. Burned eyes. She looked disgusting: weak, squirmy, blotchy, pink, like a newborn mouse. None of us wanted to look like that, ever. For a moment, even though we knew what was being done to her, we despised her.

Crybaby. Crybaby. Crybaby.

We meant it, which is the bad part.

I used to think well of myself. I didn't then.

That was last week. This week Janine doesn't wait for us to jeer at her. It was my fault, she says. It was my own fault. I led them on. I deserved the pain.

Very good, Janine, says Aunt Lydia. You are an example.

I have to wait until this is over before I put up my hand. Sometimes, if you ask at the wrong moment, they say No. If you really have to go that can be crucial. Yesterday Dolores wet the floor. Two Aunts hauled her away, a hand under each armpit. She wasn't there for the afternoon walk, but at night she was back in her usual bed. All night we could hear her moaning, off and on.

What did they do to her? we whispered, from bed to bed.

I don't know.

Not knowing makes it worse.

I raise my hand, Aunt Lydia nods. I stand up and walk out into the hall, as inconspicuously as possible. Outside the washroom Aunt Elizabeth is standing guard. She nods, signalling that I can go in.

This washroom used to be for boys. The mirrors have been replaced here too by oblongs of dull grey metal, but the urinals are still there, on one wall, white enamel with yellow stains. They look oddly like babies' coffins. I marvel again at the nakedness of men's lives: the showers right out in the open, the body exposed for inspection and comparison, the public display of privates. What is it for? What purposes of reassurance does it serve? The flashing of a badge, look, everyone, all is in order, I belong here. Why don't women have to prove to one another that they are women? Some form of unbuttoning, some split-crotch routine, just as casual. A dog-like sniffing.

The high school is old, the stalls are wooden, some kind of chipboard. I go into the second one from the end, swing the door to. Of course there are no longer any locks. In the wood there's a small hole, at the back, next to the wall, about waist height, souvenir of some previous vandalism or legacy of an ancient voyeur. Everyone in the Centre knows about this hole in the woodwork; everyone except the Aunts.

I'm afraid I am too late, held up by Janine's Testifying: maybe Moira has been here already, maybe she's had to go back. They don't give you much time. I look carefully down, aslant under the stall wall, and there are two red shoes. But how can I tell who it is?

I put my mouth to the wooden hole. Moira? I whisper.

Is that you? she says.

Yes, I say. Relief goes through me.

God, do I need a cigarette, says Moira.

Me too, I say.

I feel ridiculously happy.

I SINK DOWN into my body as into a swamp, fenland, where only I know the footing. Treacherous ground, my own territory. I become the earth I set my ear against, for rumours of the future. Each twinge, each murmur of slight pain, ripples of sloughed-off matter, swellings and diminishings of tissue, the droolings of the flesh, these are signs, these are the things I need to know about. Each month I watch for blood, fearfully, for when it comes it means failure. I have failed once again to fulfil the expectations of others, which have become my own.

I used to think of my body as an instrument, of pleasure, or a means of transportation, or an implement for the accomplishment of my will. I could use it to run, push buttons, of one sort or another, make things happen. There were limits but my body was nevertheless lithe, single, solid, one with me.

Now the flesh arranges itself differently. I'm a cloud, congealed around a central object, the shape of a pear, which is hard and more real than I am and glows red within its translucent wrapping. Inside it is a space, huge as the sky at night and dark and curved like that, though black-red rather than black. Pinpoints of light swell, sparkle, burst and shrivel within it, countless as stars. Every month there is a moon, gigantic, round, heavy, an omen. It transits, pauses, continues on and passes out of sight, and I see despair coming towards me like famine. To feel that empty, again, again. I listen to my heart, wave upon wave, salty and red, continuing on and on, marking time.

* * *

I'M IN OUR first apartment, in the bedroom. I'm standing in front of the cupboard, which has folding doors made of wood. Around me I know it's empty, all the furniture is gone, the floors are bare, no carpets even; but despite this the cupboard is full of clothes. I think they're my clothes, but they don't look like mine, I've never seen them before. Maybe they're clothes belonging to Luke's wife, whom I've also never seen; only pictures and a voice on the phone, late at night, when she was calling us, crying, accusing, before the divorce. But no, they're my clothes all right. I need a dress, I need something to wear. I pull out dresses, black, blue, purple, jackets, skirts; none of them will do, none of them even fits, they're too big or too small.

Luke is there, behind me, I turn to see him. He won't look at me, he looks down at the floor, where the cat is rubbing itself against his legs, mewing and mewing plaintively. It wants food, but how can there be any food with the apartment so empty?

Luke, I say. He doesn't answer. Maybe he doesn't hear me. It occurs to me that he may not be alive.

I'M RUNNING, WITH her, holding her hand, pulling, dragging her through the bracken, she's only half awake because of the pill I gave her, so she wouldn't cry or say anything that would give us away, she doesn't know where she is. The ground is uneven, rocks, dead branches, the smell of damp earth, old leaves, she can't run fast enough, by myself I could run faster, I'm a good runner. Now she's crying, she's frightened, I want to carry her but she would be too heavy. I have my hiking boots on and I think, when we reach the water I'll have to kick them off, will it be too cold, will she be able to swim that far, what about the current, we weren't expecting this. *Quiet*, I say to her angrily. I think about her drowning and this thought slows me. Then the shots come behind us, not loud, not like firecrackers, but sharp and crisp like a dry branch snapping. It sounds wrong, nothing ever sounds the way you think it will, and I hear the voice, *Down*, is it a real voice or a voice inside my head or my own voice, out loud?

I pull her to the ground and roll on top of her to cover her, shield her. *Quiet*, I say again, my face is wet, sweat or tears, I feel calm and floating, as if I'm no longer in my body; close to my eyes there's a leaf, red, turned early, I can see every bright vein. It's the most beautiful thing I've ever seen. I ease off, I don't want to smother her, instead I curl myself around her, keeping my hand over her mouth. There's breath and the knocking of my heart, like pounding, at the door of a house at night, where you thought you would be safe. *It's all right, I'm here*, I say, whisper, *Please be quiet*, but how can she? She's too young, it's too late, we come apart, my arms are held, and the edges go dark and nothing is left but a little window, a very little window, like the wrong end of a telescope, like the window on a Christmas card, an old one, night and ice outside, and within a candle, a shining tree, a family, I can hear the bells even, sleighbells, from the radio, old music, but through this window I can see, small but very clear, I can see her, going away from me, through the trees which are already turning, red and yellow, holding out her arms to me, being carried away.

THE BELL WAKES me; and then Cora, knocking at my door. I sit up, on the rug, wipe my wet face with my sleeve. Of all the dreams this is the worst.

Ten

WHEN THE BELL has finished I descend the stairs, a brief waif in the eye of glass that hangs on the downstairs wall. The clock ticks with its pendulum, keeping time; my feet in their neat red shoes count the way down.

The sitting-room door is wide open. I go in: so far no one else is here. I don't sit, but take my place, kneeling, near the chair with the footstool where Serena Joy will shortly enthrone herself, leaning on her cane while she lowers herself down. Possibly she'll put a hand on my shoulder, to steady herself, as if I'm a piece of furniture. She's done it before.

The sitting room would once have been called a drawing room, perhaps; then a living room. Or maybe it's a parlour, the kind with a spider and flies. But now it's officially a sitting room, because that's what is done in it, by some. For others there's standing room only. The posture of the body is important, here and now: minor discomforts are instructive.

The sitting room is subdued, symmetrical; it's one of the shapes money takes when it freezes. Money has trickled through this room for years and years, as if through an underground cavern, crusting and hardening like stalactites into these forms. Mutely the varied surfaces present themselves: the dusk-rose velvet of the drawn drapes, the gloss of the matching chairs, eighteenth century, the cow's-tongue hush of the tufted Chinese rug on the floor, with its peach-pink peonies, the suave leather of the Commander's chair, the glint of brass on the box beside it.

The rug is authentic. Some things in this room are authentic, some are not. For instance, two paintings, both of women, one on either side of the fireplace. Both wear dark dresses, like the ones in the old church, though of a later date. The paintings are possibly authentic. I suspect that when Serena Joy acquired them, after it became obvious to her that she'd have to redirect her energies into something convincingly domestic, she had the intention of passing them off as ancestors. Or maybe they were in the house when the Commander bought it. There's no way of knowing such things. In any case, there they hang, their backs and mouths stiff, their breasts constricted, their faces pinched, their caps starched, their skin greyish-white, guarding the room with their narrowed eyes.

Between them, over the mantel, there's an oval mirror, flanked by two pairs of silver candlesticks, with a white china Cupid centred between them, its arm around the neck of a lamb. The tastes of Serena Joy are a strange blend: hard lust for quality, soft sentimental cravings. There's a dried flower arrangement on either end of the mantelpiece, and a vase of real daffodils on the polished marquetry end table beside the sofa.

The room smells of lemon oil, heavy cloth, fading daffodils, the leftover smells of cooking that have made their way from the kitchen or the dining room, and of Serena Joy's perfume: Lily of the Valley. Perfume is a luxury, she must have some private source. I breathe it in, thinking I should appreciate it. It's the scent of prepubescent girls, of the gifts young children used to give their mothers, for Mother's Day; the smell of white cotton socks and white cotton petticoats, of dusting powder, of the innocence of female flesh not yet given over to hairiness and blood. It makes me feel slightly ill, as if I'm in a closed car on a hot muggy day with an older woman wearing too much face powder. This is what the sitting room is like, despite its elegance.

I would like to steal something from this room. I would like to take some small thing, the scrolled ashtray, the little silver pillbox from the mantel perhaps, or a dried flower: hide it in the folds of my dress or in my zippered sleeve, keep it there until this evening is over, secrete it in my room, under the bed, or in a shoe, or in a slit in the hard petit-point FAITH cushion. Every once in a while I would take it out and look at it. It would make me feel that I have power.

But such a feeling would be an illusion, and too risky. My hands stay where they are, folded in my lap. Thighs together, heels tucked underneath me, pressing up against my body. Head lowered. In my mouth there's the taste of toothpaste: fake mint and plaster.

I wait, for the household to assemble. *Household*: that is what we are. The Commander is the head of the household. The house is what he holds. To have and to hold, till death do us part.

The hold of a ship. Hollow.

Cora comes in first, then Rita, wiping her hands on her apron. They too have been summoned by the bell, they resent it, they have other things to do, the dishes for instance. But they need to be here, they all need to be here, the Ceremony demands it. We are all obliged to sit through this, one way or another.

Rita scowls at me before slipping in to stand behind me. It's my fault, this waste of her time. Not mine, but my body's, if there is a difference. Even the Commander is subject to its whims.

Nick walks in, nods to all three of us, looks around the room. He too takes his place behind me, standing. He's so close that the tip of his boot is touching my foot. Is this on purpose? Whether it is or not we are touching, two shapes of leather. I feel my shoe soften, blood flows into it, it grows warm, it becomes a skin. I move my foot slightly, away.

'Wish he'd hurry up,' says Cora.

'Hurry up and wait,' says Nick. He laughs, moves his foot so it's touching mine again. No one can see, beneath the folds of my outspread skirt. I shift, it's too warm in here, the smell of stale perfume makes me feel a little sick. I move my foot away.

We hear Serena coming, down the stairs, along the hall, the muffled tap of her cane on the rug, thud of the good foot. She hobbles through the doorway, glances at us, counting but not seeing. She nods, at Nick, but says nothing. She's in one of her best dresses, sky-blue with embroidery in white along the edges of the veil: flowers and fretwork. Even at her age she still feels the urge to wreathe herself in flowers. No use for you, I think at her, my face unmoving, you can't use them any more, you're withered. They're the genital organs of plants. I read that somewhere, once.

She makes her way to her chair and footstool, turns, lowers herself, lands ungracefully. She hoists her left foot onto the stool, fumbles in her sleeve pocket. I can hear the rustling, the click of her lighter, I smell the hot singe of the smoke, breathe it in.

'Late as usual,' she says. We don't answer. There's a clatter as she gropes on the lamp table, then a click, and the television set runs through its warm-up.

A male choir, with greenish-yellow skin, the colour needs adjusting, they're singing 'Come to the Church in the Wildwood.' *Come, come, come, come*, sing the basses. Serena clicks the channel changer. Waves, coloured zigzags, a garble of sound: it's the Montreal satellite station, being blocked. Then there's a preacher, earnest, with shining dark eyes, leaning towards us across a desk. These days they look a lot like businessmen. Serena gives him a few seconds, then clicks onward.

Several blank channels, then the news. This is what she's been looking for. She leans back, inhales deeply. I on the contrary lean forward, a child being allowed up late with the grown-ups. This is the one good thing about these evenings, the evenings of the Ceremony: I'm allowed to watch the news. It seems to be an unspoken rule in this household: we always get here on time, he's always late, Serena always lets us watch the news.

Such as it is: who knows if any of it is true? It could be old clips, it could be faked. But I watch it anyway, hoping to be able to read beneath it. Any news, now, is better than none.

First, the front lines. They are not lines, really: the war seems to be going on in many places at once.

Wooded hills, seen from above, the trees a sickly yellow. I wish she'd fix the colour. The Appalachian Highlands, says the voice-over, where the Angels of the Apocalypse, Fourth Division, are smoking out a pocket of Baptist guerrillas, with air support from the Twenty-first Battalion of the Angels of Light. We are shown two helicopters, black ones with silver wings painted on the sides. Below them, a clump of trees explodes.

Now a close shot of a prisoner, with a stubbled and dirty face, flanked by two Angels in their neat black uniforms. The prisoner accepts a cigarette from one of the Angels, puts it awkwardly to his lips with his bound hands. He gives a lopsided little grin. The announcer is saying something, but I don't hear it: I look into this man's eyes, trying to decide what he's thinking. He knows the camera is on him: is the grin a show of defiance, or is it submission? Is he embarrassed, at having been caught?

They show us only victories, never defeats. Who wants bad news?

Possibly he's an actor.

The anchorman comes on now. His manner is kindly, fatherly; he gazes out at us from the screen, looking, with his tan and his white hair and candid eyes, wise wrinkles around them, like everybody's ideal grandfather. What he's telling us, his level smile implies, is for our own good. Everything will be all right soon. I promise. There will be peace. You must trust. You must go to sleep, like good children.

He tells us what we long to believe. He's very convincing.

I struggle against him. He's like an old movie star, I tell myself, with false teeth and a face job. At the same time I sway towards him, like one hypnotized. If only it were true. If only I could believe.

Now he's telling us that an underground espionage ring has been cracked, by a team of Eyes, working with an inside informant. The ring has been smuggling precious national resources over the border into Canada.

'Five members of the heretical sect of Quakers have

been arrested,' he says, smiling blandly, 'and more arrests are anticipated.'

Two of the Quakers appear onscreen, a man and a woman. They look terrified, but they're trying to preserve some dignity in front of the camera. The man has a large dark mark on his forehead; the woman's veil has been torn off, and her hair falls in strands over her face. Both of them are about fifty.

Now we can see a city, again from the air. This used to be Detroit. Under the voice of the announcer there's the thunk of artillery. From the skyline columns of smoke ascend.

'Resettlement of the Children of Ham is continuing on schedule,' says the reassuring pink face, back on the screen. 'Three thousand have arrived this week in National Homeland One, with another two thousand in transit.' How are they transporting that many people at once? Trains, buses? We are not shown any pictures of this. National Homeland One is in North Dakota. Lord knows what they're supposed to do, once they get there. Farm, is the theory.

Serena Joy has had enough of the news. Impatiently she clicks the button for a station change, comes up with an aging bass baritone, his cheeks like emptied udders. 'Whispering Hope' is what he's singing. Serena turns him off.

We wait, the clock in the hall ticks, Serena lights another cigarette, I get into the car. It's a Saturday morning, it's a September, we still have a car. Other people have had to sell theirs. My name isn't Offred, I have another name, which nobody uses now because it's forbidden. I tell myself it doesn't matter, your name is like your telephone number, useful only to others; but what I tell myself is wrong, it does matter. I keep the knowledge of this name like something hidden, some treasure I'll come back to dig up, one day. I think of this name as buried. This name has an aura around it, like an amulet, some charm that's survived from an unimaginably distant past. I lie in my single bed at night, with my eyes closed, and the name floats there behind my eyes, not quite within reach, shining in the dark.

It's a Saturday morning in September, I'm wearing my shining name. The little girl who is now dead sits in the back seat, with her two best dolls, her stuffed rabbit, mangy with age and love. I know all the details. They are sentimental details but I can't help that. I can't think about the rabbit too much though, I can't start to cry, here on the Chinese rug, breathing in the smoke that has been inside Serena's body. Not here, not now, I can do that later.

She thought we were going on a picnic, and in fact there is a picnic basket on the back seat, beside her, with real food in it, hard-boiled eggs, thermos and all. We didn't want her to know where we were really going, we didn't want her to tell, by mistake, reveal anything, if we were stopped. We didn't want to lay upon her the burden of our truth.

I wore my hiking boots, she had on her sneakers. The

laces of the sneakers had a design of hearts on them, red, purple, pink, and yellow. It was warm for the time of year, the leaves were turning already, some of them; Luke drove, I sat beside him, the sun shone, the sky was blue, the houses as we passed them looked comforting and ordinary, each house as it was left behind vanishing into past time, crumbling in an instant as if it had never been, because I would never see it again, or so I thought then.

We have almost nothing with us, we don't want to look as if we're going anywhere far or permanent. We have the forged passports, guaranteed, worth the price. We couldn't pay in money, of course, or put it on the Compucount: we used other things, some jewellery that was my grandmother's, a stamp collection Luke inherited from his uncle. Such things can be exchanged, for money, in other countries. When we get to the border we'll pretend we're just going over on a day trip; the fake visas are for a day. Before that I'll give her a sleeping pill so she'll be asleep when we cross. That way she won't betray us. You can't expect a child to lie convincingly.

And I don't want her to feel frightened, to feel the fear that is now tightening my muscles, tensing my spine, pulling me so taut that I'm certain I would break if touched. Every stop-light is an ordeal. We'll spend the night at a motel, or, better, sleeping in the car on a sideroad so there will be no suspicious questions. We'll cross in the morning, drive over the bridge, easily, just like driving to the supermarket.

We turn onto the freeway, head north, flowing with not much traffic. Since the war started, gas is expensive and in short supply. Outside the city we pass the first checkpoint. All they want is a look at the licence, Luke does it well. The licence matches the passport: we thought of that.

Back on the road, he squeezes my hand, glances over at me. You're white as a sheet, he says.

That is how I feel: white, flat, thin. I feel transparent. Surely they will be able to see through me. Worse, how will I be able to hold on to Luke, to her, when I'm so flat, so white? I feel as if there's not much left of me; they will slip through my arms, as if I'm made of smoke, as if I'm a mirage, fading before their eyes. *Don't think that way,* Moira would say. *Think that way and you'll make it happen.*

Cheer up, says Luke. He's driving a little too fast now. The adrenalin's gone to his head. Now he's singing. Oh what a beautiful morning, he sings.

Even his singing worries me. We've been warned not to look too happy.

Eleven

THE COMMANDER KNOCKS at the door. The knock is prescribed: the sitting room is supposed to be Serena Joy's territory, he's supposed to ask permission to enter it. She likes to keep him waiting. It's a little thing, but in this household little things mean a lot. Tonight, however, she doesn't even get that, because before Serena Joy can speak he steps forward into the room anyway. Maybe he's just forgotten the protocol, but maybe it's deliberate. Who knows what she said to him, over the silver-encrusted dinner table? Or didn't say.

The Commander has on his black uniform, in which he looks like a museum guard. A semi-retired man, genial but wary, killing time. But only at first glance. After that he looks like a midwestern bank president, with his straight neatly brushed silver hair, his sober posture, shoulders a little stooped. And after that there is his moustache, silver also, and after that his chin, which really you can't miss. When you get down as far as the chin he looks like a vodka ad, in a glossy magazine, of times gone by.

His manner is mild, his hands large, with thick fingers and acquisitive thumbs, his blue eyes uncommunicative, falsely innocuous. He looks us over as if taking inventory. One kneel-woman in red, one seated woman in blue, two in green, standing, a solitary man, thin-faced, in the background. He manages to appear puzzled, as if he can't quite remember how we all got in here. As if we are something he inherited, like a Victorian pump organ, and he hasn't figured out what to do with us. What we are worth.

He nods, in the general direction of Serena Joy, who does not make a sound. He crosses to the large leather chair reserved for him, takes the key out of his pocket, fumbles with the ornate brass-bound leather-covered box that stands on the table beside the chair. He inserts the key, opens the box, lifts out the Bible, an ordinary copy, with a black cover and gold-edged pages. The Bible is kept locked up, the way people once kept tea locked up, so the servants wouldn't steal it. It is an incendiary device: who knows what we'd make of it, if we ever got our hands on it? We can be read to from it, by him, but we cannot read. Our heads turn towards him, we are expectant, here comes our bedtime story.

The Commander sits down and crosses his legs, watched by us. The bookmarks are in place. He opens the book. He clears his throat a little, as if embarrassed.

'Could I have a drink of water?' he says to the air. 'Please,' he adds.

Behind me, one of them, Cora or Rita, leaves her space in the tableau and pads off towards the kitchen. The Commander sits, looking down. The Commander sighs, takes out a pair of reading glasses from his inside jacket pocket, gold rims, slips them on. Now he looks like a shoemaker in an old fairytale book. Is there no end to his disguises, of benevolence?

We watch him: every inch, every flicker.

To be a man, watched by women. It must be entirely strange. To have them watching him all the time. To have them wondering, What's he going to do next? To have them flinch when he moves, even if it's a harmless enough move, to reach for an ashtray perhaps. To have them sizing him up. To have them thinking, he can't do it, he won't do, he'll have to do, this last as if he were a garment, out of style or shoddy, which must nevertheless be put on because there's nothing else available.

To have them putting him on, trying him on, trying him out, while he himself puts them on, like a sock over a foot, onto the stub of himself, his extra, sensitive thumb, his tentacle, his delicate stalked slug's eye, which extrudes, expands, winces, and shrivels back into himself when touched wrongly, grows big again, bulging a little at the tip, travelling forward as if along a leaf, into them, avid for vision. To achieve vision in this way, this journey into a darkness that is composed of women, a woman, who can see in darkness while he himself strains blindly forward.

She watches him from within. We're all watching him. It's one thing we can really do, and it's not for nothing: if he were to falter, fail or die, what would become of us? No wonder he's like a boot, hard on the outside, giving shape to a pulp of tenderfoot. That's just a wish. I've been watching him for some time and he's given no evidence, of softness.

But watch out, Commander, I tell him in my head. I've got my eye on you. One false move and I'm dead.

Still, it must be hell, to be a man, like that.

It must be just fine.

It must be hell.

It must be very silent.

THE WATER APPEARS, the Commander drinks it. 'Thank you,' he says. Cora rustles back into place.

The Commander pauses, looking down, scanning the page. He takes his time, as if unconscious of us. He's like a man toying with a steak, behind a restaurant window, pretending not to see the eyes watching him from hungry darkness not three feet from his elbow. We lean towards him a little, iron filings to his magnet. He has something we don't have, he has the word. How we squandered it, once.

The Commander, as if reluctantly, begins to read. He isn't very good at it. Maybe he's merely bored.

It's the usual story, the usual stories. God to Adam, God to Noah. *Be fruitful, and multiply, and replenish the earth.* Then comes the mouldy old Rachel and Leah stuff we had drummed into us at the Centre. *Give me children, or else I die. Am I in God's stead, who hath withheld from thee the fruit of the womb? Behold my maid Bilhah. She shall bear upon my knees, that I may also have children by her.* And so on and so forth. We had it read to us every breakfast, as we sat in the high-school cafeteria, eating porridge with cream and brown sugar. You're getting the best, you know, said Aunt Lydia. There's a war on, things are rationed. You are spoiled girls, she twinkled, as if rebuking a kitten. Naughty puss.

FOR LUNCH IT was the Beatitudes. Blessed be this, blessed be that. They played it from a disc, the voice was a man's. *Blessed be the poor in spirit, for theirs is the kingdom of heaven. Blessed are the merciful. Blessed are the meek. Blessed are the silent.* I knew they made that up, I knew it was wrong, and they left things out too, but there was no way of checking. *Blessed be those that mourn, for they shall be comforted.*

Nobody said when.

I check the clock, during dessert, canned pears with cinnamon, standard for lunch, and look for Moira in her place, two tables over. She's gone already. I put my hand up, I am excused. We don't do this too often, and always at different times of day.

In the washroom I go to the second-last stall, as usual.

Are you there? I whisper.

Large as life and twice as ugly, Moira whispers back.

What have you heard? I ask her.

Nothing much. I've got to get out of here, I'm going bats.

I feel panic. No, no, Moira, I say, don't try it. Not on your own.

I'll fake sick. They send an ambulance, I've seen it.

You'll only get as far as the hospital.

At least it'll be a change. I won't have to listen to that old bitch.

They'll find you out.

Not to worry, I'm good at it. When I was a kid in high school I cut out vitamin C, I got scurvy. In the early stages they can't diagnose it. Then you just start it again and you're fine. I'll hide my vitamin pills.

Moira, don't.

I couldn't stand the thought of her not being here, with me. For me.

They send two guys with you, in the ambulance. Think about it. They must be starved for it, shit, they aren't even allowed to put their hands in their pockets, the possibilities are –

You in there. Time's up, said the voice of Aunt Elizabeth, from the doorway. I stood up, flushed the toilet. Two of Moira's fingers appeared, through the hole in the wall. It was only large enough for two fingers. I touched my own fingers to them, quickly, held on. Let go.

* * *

'And Leah said, God hath given me my hire, because I have given my maiden to my husband,' says the Commander. He lets the book fall closed. It makes an exhausted sound, like a padded door shutting, by itself, at a distance: a puff of air. The sound suggests the softness of the thin oniony pages, how they would feel under the fingers. Soft and dry, like *papier poudre*, pink and powdery, from the time before, you'd get it in booklets for taking the shine off your nose, in those stores that sold candles and soap in the shapes of things: seashells, mushrooms. Like cigarette paper. Like petals.

The Commander sits with his eyes closed for a moment, as if tired. He works long hours. He has a lot of responsibilities.

Serena has begun to cry. I can hear her, behind my back. It isn't the first time. She always does this, the night of the Ceremony. She's trying not to make a noise. She's trying to preserve her dignity, in front of us. The upholstery and the rugs muffle her but we can hear her clearly despite that. The tension between her lack of control and her attempt to suppress it is horrible. It's like a fart in church. I feel, as always, the urge to laugh, but not because I think it's funny. The smell of her crying spreads over us and we pretend to ignore it.

The Commander opens his eyes, notices, frowns, ceases to notice. 'Now we will have a moment of silent prayer,' says the Commander. 'We will ask for a blessing, and for success in all our ventures.'

I bow my head and close my eyes. I listen to the held breath, the almost inaudible gasps, the shaking going on behind my back. How she must hate me, I think.

I PRAY SILENTLY: *Nolite te bastardes carborundorum.* I don't know what it means, but it sounds right, and it will have to do, because I don't know what else I can say to God. Not right now. Not, as they used to say, at this juncture. The scratched writing on my cupboard wall floats before me, left by an unknown woman, with the face of Moira. I saw her go out, to the ambulance, on a stretcher, carried by two Angels.

What is it? I mouthed to the woman beside me; safe enough, a question like that, to all but a fanatic.

A fever, she formed with her lips. Appendicitis, they say.

I was having dinner, that evening, hamburger balls and hashed browns. My table was near the window, I could see out, as far as the front gates. I saw the ambulance come back, no siren this time. One of the Angels jumped out, talked with the guard. The guard went into the building; the ambulance stayed parked; the Angel stood with his back towards us, as they had been taught to do. Two of the Aunts came out of the building, with the guard. They went around to the back. They hauled Moira out, dragged her in through the gate and up the front steps, holding her under the armpits, one on each side. She was having trouble walking. I stopped eating, I couldn't eat; by this time all of us on my side of the table were staring out the window. The window was greenish, with that chicken-wire mesh they used to put inside glass. Aunt Lydia said, Eat your dinner. She went over and pulled down the blind.

They took her into a room that used to be the Science Lab. It was a room where none of us ever went willingly. Afterwards she could not walk for a week, her feet would not fit into her shoes, they were too swollen. It was the feet they'd do, for a first offence. They used steel cables, frayed at the ends. After that the hands. They didn't care what they did to your feet and hands, even if it was permanent. Remember, said Aunt Lydia. For our purposes your feet and your hands are not essential.

Moira lay on her bed, an example. She shouldn't have tried it, not with the Angels, Alma said, from the next bed over. We had to carry her to classes. We stole extra paper packets of sugar for her, from the cafeteria at mealtimes, smuggled them to her, at night, handing them from bed to bed. Probably she didn't need the sugar but it was the only thing we could find to steal. To give.

I am still praying but what I am seeing is Moira's feet, the way they looked after they'd brought her back. Her feet did not look like feet at all. They looked like drowned feet, swollen and boneless, except for the colour. They looked like lungs.

Oh God, I pray. *Nolite te bastardes carborundorum.*

Is this what you had in mind?

* * *

THE COMMANDER CLEARS his throat. This is what he does to let us know that in his opinion it's time we stopped praying. 'For the eyes of the Lord run to and fro throughout the whole earth, to know himself strong in the behalf of them whose heart is perfect towards him,' he says.

It's the sign-off. He stands up. We are dismissed.

Twelve

THE CEREMONY GOES as usual.

I lie on my back, fully clothed except for the healthy white cotton underdrawers. What I could see, if I were to open my eyes, would be the large white canopy of Serena Joy's outsized colonial-style four-poster bed, suspended like a sagging cloud above us, a cloud sprigged with tiny drops of silver rain, which, if you looked at them closely, would turn out to be four-petalled flowers. I would not see the carpet, which is white, or the sprigged curtains and skirted dressing table with its silver-backed brush and mirror set; only the canopy, which manages to suggest at one and the same time, by the gauziness of its fabric and its heavy downward curve, both ethereality and matter.

Or the sail of a ship. Big-bellied sails, they used to say, in poems. Bellying. Propelled forward by a swollen belly.

A mist of Lily of the Valley surrounds us, chilly, crisp almost. It's not warm in this room.

Above me, towards the head of the bed, Serena Joy is arranged, outspread. Her legs are apart, I lie between them, my head on her stomach, her pubic bone under the base of my skull, her thighs on either side of me. She too is fully clothed.

My arms are raised; she holds my hands, each of mine in each of hers. This is supposed to signify that we are one flesh, one being. What it really means is that she is in control, of the process and thus of the product. If any. The rings of her left hand cut into my fingers. It may or may not be revenge.

My red skirt is hitched up to my waist, though no higher. Below it the Commander is fucking. What he is fucking is the lower part of my body. I do not say making love, because this is not what he's doing. Copulating too would be inaccurate, because it would imply two people and only one is involved. Nor does rape cover it: nothing is going on here that I haven't signed up for. There wasn't a lot of choice but there was some, and this is what I chose.

Therefore I lie still and picture the unseen canopy over my head. I remember Queen Victoria's advice to her daughter. *Close your eyes and think of England*. But this is not England. I wish he would hurry up.

Maybe I'm crazy and this is some new kind of therapy.

I wish it were true; then I could get better and this would go away.

Serena Joy grips my hands as if it is she, not I, who's being fucked, as if she finds it either pleasurable or painful, and the Commander fucks, with a regular two-four marching stroke, on and on like a tap dripping. He is preoccupied, like a man humming to himself in the shower without knowing he's humming; like a man who has other things on his mind. It's as if he's somewhere else, waiting for himself to come, drumming his fingers on the table while he waits. There's an impatience in his rhythm now. But isn't this everyone's wet dream, two women at once? They used to say that. Exciting, they used to say.

What's going on in this room, under Serena Joy's silvery canopy, is not exciting. It has nothing to do with passion or love or romance or any of those other notions we used to titillate ourselves with. It has nothing to do with sexual desire, at least for me, and certainly not for Serena. Arousal and orgasm are no longer thought necessary; they would be a symptom of frivolity merely, like jazz garters or beauty spots: superfluous distractions for the light-minded. Outdated. It seems odd that women once spent such time and energy reading about such things, thinking about them, worrying about them, writing about them. They are so obviously recreational.

This is not recreation, even for the Commander. This is serious business. The Commander, too, is doing his duty.

If I were to open my eyes a slit, I would be able to see him, his not-unpleasant face hanging over my torso, with a few strands of his silver hair falling perhaps over his forehead, intent on his inner journey, that place he is hurrying towards, which recedes as in a dream at the same speed with which he approaches it. I would see his open eyes.

If he were better looking would I enjoy this more?

At least he's an improvement on the previous one, who smelled like a church cloakroom in the rain; like your mouth when the dentist starts picking at your teeth; like a nostril. The Commander, instead, smells of mothballs, or is this odour some punitive form of aftershave? Why does he have to wear that stupid uniform? But would I like his white, tufted raw body any better?

Kissing is forbidden between us. This makes it bearable.

One detaches oneself. One describes.

He comes at last, with a stifled groan as of relief Serena Joy, who has been holding her breath, expels it. The Commander, who has been propping himself on his elbows, away from our combined bodies, doesn't permit himself to sink down into us. He rests a moment, withdraws, recedes, rezippers. He nods, then turns and leaves the room, closing the door with exaggerated care behind him, as if both of us are his ailing mother. There's something hilarious about this, but I don't dare laugh.

Serena Joy lets go of my hands. 'You can get up now,' she says. 'Get up and get out.' She's supposed to have me rest, for ten minutes, with my feet on a pillow to improve the chances. This is meant to be a time of silent meditation for her, but she's not in the mood for that. There is loathing in her voice, as if the touch of my flesh sickens and contaminates her. I untangle myself from her body, stand up; the juice of the Commander runs down my legs. Before I turn away I see her straighten her blue skirt, clench her legs together; she continues lying on the bed, gazing up at the canopy above her, stiff and straight as an effigy.

Which of us is it worse for, her or me?

From *Hag-Seed*

UNCEREMONIOUSLY OUSTED FROM his role as Artistic Director at the Makeshiweg Theatre Festival, Felix – or Mr. Duke, as he's known – takes up a post teaching a Shakespeare theatre course at the Fletcher Correctional Institute. This year the play he chooses to direct and broadcast on the prison's televisions is *The Tempest.* Afterwards, the prisoner/actors wonder, 'What happens to Hag-Seed/Caliban after the end of the play?' And we readers wonder: 'What is freedom?'

FELIX STANDS BESIDE the whiteboard at the front of the large main room, facing this year's class. Although he's read the signup list and sent out the course packages – the playbook, the notes – he never knows ahead of time who will actually show up. There are always some drop-outs, and thus some replacements from the waiting list. To his credit there's always a waiting list. There can be absences for other reasons too. Transfers to other facilities, early paroles, injuries requiring infirmary time.

He scans the room. Familiar faces, veterans of his previous plays: these nod at him, offer half-smiles. New faces, blank or apprehensive: they don't know what to expect. Lost boys all of them, though they are not boys: their ages range from nineteen to forty-five. They are many hues, from white to black through yellow, red, and brown; they are many ethnicities. The crimes for which they've been convicted are assorted. The one thing they share, apart from their imprisoned state, is a desire to be in Felix's acting troupe. Their motives, he expects, are varied.

He's read their files, obtained for him by Estelle through some mysterious process, although he pretends he hasn't; so he knows what they're in here for. Some are gang members taking the rap for a higher-up, some have been busted for semi-amateur drug-dealing. Theft, from banks to break-and-enters to cars to convenience stores. A boy-genius hacker, convicted as a for-hire purloiner of corporate information. A con man and identity-theft specialist. A renegade doctor. An accountant from a respectable firm, doing time for embezzlement. A lawyer and Ponzi scheme scammer.

Some of them are seasoned actors, having been in several of his plays. Technically they shouldn't be able to take the course more than once, but Felix has sidestepped this stricture by adding a few spinoffs to his main offering, with how-tos and plug-ins downloaded from the Net. In 'Technology for the Theatre,' they learn lighting, props, special effects, and digital scenery. In 'Theatre Design,' they learn costume, makeup, wigs, and masks. In 'Video Editing for the Theatre,' they learn how to make silk purses out of sows' ears. He doles out academic credits accordingly. It all looks good on paper to the powers that be. Mr. Duke is such a bargain: four courses for the price of one.

Meanwhile he's nurtured a number of skill sets he can call upon when needed. He's got costume designers, he's got video editors, he's got lighting and special-effects men, he's got tip-top disguise artists. He does sometimes wonder how the crafts he's teaching might come in handy in, for instance, a bank robbery or a kidnapping, but he backgrounds such unworthy thoughts when they appear.

He gazes around the room, already casting the roles in his head. There's his perfect Ferdinand, Prince of Naples, gazing at him with round, ingenuous eyes as if ready to fall in love: WonderBoy, the con artist. There's his Ariel, unless he's much mistaken, elemental air spirit, slender and adroit, scintillating with cool juvenile intelligence: 8Handz, genius black-hat hacker. A podgy Gonzalo, the boring, worthy councillor: Bent Pencil, the warped accountant. And Antonio, the magician Prospero's treacherous, usurping brother: SnakeEye, the Ponzi schemer and real-estate fraudster, with his slanted left eye and lop-sided mouth that make him look as if he's sneering.

A moon-calf Trinculo, the fool, the jester. No obvious Stephano, the drunken butler. Various Calibans, scowling and muscular: earthy, potentially violent. He'll have a choice. But before making up his mind about any of them he'll have to hear them speak some lines.

He smiles confidently, the smile of someone who knows what he's doing. Then he launches into a version of the speech with which he begins every new season.

'Good morning,' he says. 'Welcome to the Fletcher Correctional Players. I don't care why you're in here or what they say you've done: for this course the past is prologue, which means we begin counting time and accomplishments right here, right now.

'As of this moment, you are actors. You will all be acting in a play; everyone will have a function, as the old hands who've done it before will tell you. The Fletcher Correctional Players only do plays by Shakespeare, because that is the best and most complete way of learning theatre. Shakespeare has something for everyone, because that's who his audience was: everyone, from high to low and back again.

'My name is Mr. Duke, and I'm the director. That means I'm in charge of the overall production, and the final say is mine.

'But we work as a team. Each man will have an essential part to perform, and if someone's having trouble it's the job of his teammates to help him out, because our play will be only as strong as the weakest link: if one of us fails, we all fail together. So if a guy on your team has trouble reading the words, you need to help him. And you need to help each other memorize the parts, and understand what the words mean and how to deliver them with force. That's your mission. We must all rise to the highest level. The Fletcher Correctional Players have a reputation to live up to, and what we create together will honour that reputation.

'You've heard me mention teams, and those of you who've been in one of my plays before know what that means. Each of the principal characters will have a team surrounding him, and everyone on that team must learn that character's speeches. That's because each main actor must have some understudies, in case of illness or any other . . . in case of unforeseen emergencies, such as early parole, for instance. Or a slip in the shower room. The play must go on despite everything: that's how it is in the theatre. In this company, we back each other up.

'You'll be doing some writing. You'll be writing about aspects of the play, but you'll also be rewriting those parts of the play you decide – we decide – could be made more understandable to a modern audience. We'll be filming a video of our production; that video gets screened for everyone in the – for everyone in Fletcher. Our video will be something to be proud of, as our previous productions have been.'

He smiles reassuringly, consults a folder. 'Next, you'll need to choose a stage name. Many actors in the past did that, and opera singers and magicians as well. Harry Houdini was born Erik Weisz, Bob Dylan was Robert Zimmerman, Stevie Wonder was Steveland Judkins.' He's looked these names up on the Internet, searching *stage-alter egos*. He knows only some of them: he adds a few younger ones each time he gives this speech. 'Movie stars do it, not to mention rockers and rappers. Snoop Dog was Calvin Broadus. You see what I mean? So think up your stage name. It's like a handle.'

There are nods and murmurs. The seasoned actors already have their stage names from earlier productions.

They're smiling now: they welcome the return of this other self of theirs, standing there like a costume, ready for them to assume.

Felix pauses, steels himself for the hard sell. 'Now. This year's play.' He writes on the whiteboard, using a red marker: THE TEMPEST. 'So,' he says. 'You've been given the playbook in advance, you've got my notes, you've had time to read up on it.' For a few of them this is true only in a manner of speaking, since they're third-grade level at best. They'll improve, however: their team will improve them. They'll be hauled up the stairs of literacy step by step.

'I'll start with the keynotes,' Felix continues. 'These are the important things to look for when we're figuring out how to present this play.'

Using the blue marker, he writes:

IT'S A MUSICAL: Has the most music + songs in Shkspr. Music used for what?

MAGIC: Used for what?

PRISONS: How many?

MONSTERS: Who is one?

REVENGE: Who wants it? Why?

Consulting their faces – stony, frowning, or blankly bewildered – he thinks: they don't get it. Not like *Julius Caesar*, not like *Macbeth*; they saw the point of those right away. Not even like *Richard III*, which had posed a challenge, since a few too many of them had sided with Richard.

He takes a deep breath. 'Off the top, any questions?'

'Yeah,' says Leggs. Break-and-enter, assault. He's a veteran of the Fletcher Correctional stage, having played Mark Antony in *Julius Caesar*, one of the witches in *Macbeth*, and Clarence in *Richard III*. 'We read it. But why're we doing this one? There's no fight scene, and it's got, like, a fairy in it.'

* * *

Two weeks to go before the day the planets converge and the tempest is unleashed. They've now recorded the initial tempest scene, with the sinking boat and 8Handz in the bathing cap and goggles: it filmed surprisingly well. Felix will do his own first scene with Ariel next week. 8Handz has been so busy with the tech that he needs more time on the lines.

Today they're shooting Caliban. They'll do the close-ups of his speeches, add the far shots later. This is the first day Leggs has been in full costume: the scaly Godzilla headgear, its eyes and teeth obliterated, its edges altered to hang in tatters around his face; his face itself mudded with makeup; lizard-skin patterns on his legs, temporary tattoos of spiders and scorpions covering his arms. It's no worse than some other Caliban outfits Felix has seen, and better than some.

'Ready?' says Felix.

'Yeah,' says Leggs. 'Um, we added something. Anne-Marie helped us with it.'

Felix turns to Anne-Marie. 'Is this any good? We can't fool around, we're running out of time, we need to get on with it.' He did encourage them to write their own extra material, so he's not entitled to be grumpy.

'Three and a half minutes,' she says. 'I timed it. And yes, it's terrific! Would I lie to you?'

'I won't answer that,' says Felix.

'Take One,' says TimEEz. 'Hag-Seed. By Caliban and the Hag-Seeds. First there's an Announcer bit, we can shoot that later. "Here comes Caliban, From his prison in a stone, Kept in slavery, Made to groan, But come what may, He got to have his own say!" Like that.'

Felix nods. 'Fine,' he says.

'Don't forget to breathe,' Anne-Marie says to Leggs. 'From the diaphragm. Remember what I said about anger. It's like fuel – find it, use it! This is your chance to roar! Take off like a rocket! One, two, go!'

Leggs rears up, crouches, shakes a fist. TimEEz, PPod, VaMoose, and Red Coyote stand off to the side, clapping out the beat, adding a soft Uh-oh, Uh-oh in syncopation, while Leggs does his chant, his rant.

My name's Caliban, got scales and long nails,
I smell like a fish and not like a man –
But my other name's Hag-Seed, or that's what he call me;
He call me a lotta names, he play me a lotta games:

He call me a poison, a filth, a slave,
He prison me up to make me behave,
But I'm Hag-Seed!

My mom's name was Sycorax, they call her a witch,
A blue-eyed hag and real bad bitch;
My daddy was the devil, or that's their story,
So I'm two times evil and I ain't never sorry,
'Cause I'm Hag-Seed!

They dump her on an island, 'cause she was up the spout,
They leave her there to croak, wasn't no joke,
I get born, she gets dead, so the island is *my* land,
This place was my kingdom! And I was the king!
I was the king of everything:
King Hag-Seed!

Then along come Prospero, his little baby bitch,
He think he something 'cause he once was rich;
At first it was good,
I showed him all the food,
He made me a pet, now this is what I get,
'Cause I tried to jump that girl, no other man to do it,
Would'a done her a favour, made a whole population,
An island nation, all Hag-Seeds!

So he pinch me black and he pinch me blue,
I got to do the work while he lies around snorin',

Or talkin' his magic, he is so borin',
I curse him back but he pinch me more,
I one big cramp, I am so sore,
But I'm Hag-Seed!

So if I get the chance I'll rip up his book,
Break his magic staff, that would be a laugh,
Bash in his brains, pay him back for my pains,
Make that girl be my Hag-Seed queen,
No matter how she scream,
The more she scream, she askin' for it,
Down on her knees, I'll make her adore it,
No matter how she whine, I'll hump her blind,
'Cause I'm Hag-Seed!

Just keep it in mind:
I'm Hag-Seed!

* * *

LEGGS MAKES HIS way up to the front of the room, red in the face and more freckled than ever. He's giving it his best shot, taking a dominant stance, one leg forward, foot angled out, then a tilt of the pelvis and the other leg swinging as if welded at the knee. He surveys the assembled cast and crew, scowling his Caliban scowl. Then he slowly rolls up his sleeves.

Good theatre, thinks Felix. He's making them wait.

'Team Hag-Seed reporting here, sir,' he says to Felix. The mode is quasi-military but at the same time subtly mocking.

'Here's the real clear truth,' he begins. 'Hag-Seed, I mean Caliban – nobody's on his team. Even his so-called friends and allies, those two drunk assholes – they're not loyal to him, they make fun of him and call him names, they're out to make a buck off him. So inside the play, he don't have a team. His only team he ever had is dead, which was his mother, who other people called a witch.

But she must've loved him enough to at least not drown him like a kitten. She did the bare essentials, she kept him alive. You gotta hand it to her, considering. She was all alone on the island, birthing the baby and so forth.

'she maybe had her failings, but she did what she could for him. She was tough.'

Nods from the audience: tough though fallible mothers are being remembered.

'Then she died and Caliban grew up on his own. He was welcoming to Prospero at first, but now Prospero's on his back 24/7, and Ariel's not gonna help him out either, though they're both slaves in a manner of speaking. They're both kept in line by threats of torture; only difference is, Ariel sucks up and Caliban holds out, so it's only Caliban who gets the pinches and cramps.

'But I'm glad to say I have a team helping me with this report, and that is the Hag-Seed backup group and costume designers for the numbers we did, namely PPod, TimEEz, VaMoose, and Red Coyote. You guys were great, I couldn't of done it without you, we really scored, and this will always be a great memory in my life.' He pauses. Is it a studied pause or is he choking up? I've taught him too well, thinks Felix, if even I can't tell the difference.

'So this is our report,' says Leggs. 'Report of Team Hag-Seed. What happens to Caliban after it's over? At the end of the play he's left dangling, so we don't really know. He's going to be a good servant to Prospero, or what?

'Okay, we thought of various ways it could of gone. First, Caliban's left on the island and the rest of them sail away. He gets the island and he's the king of it, like he wanted, but there's nobody else on it any more, so what's the point? You can't be a king unless you're the king of somebody else, right?'

Nods from the cast. They're listening intently: they really care what happens to Caliban.

'Okay, so we tossed out that one. Next – that's number two – he sails on the ship for Naples with the rest of them. Prospero gets killed and Miranda gets raped, like in what Team Antonio said – sorry, Anne-Marie, but in real life there wouldn't be any goddesses, so that's what would happen – only she's not raped by Hag-Seed. It's only by Antonio, because he's so evil, like he said. After that he kills her because he wants to be the Duke and he can't have any rivals, so she has to go, it makes sense. Caliban's pissed off by that, but he can't do nothing because by this time Stephano and Trinculo have him chained him up in the bottom of the ship.

'When they get to Naples, they put him on show for money, just like they said they would. They tell folks he's a savage from the jungle, a part-fish monster, and also he eats people. Everyone throws things at him like a gorilla in a cage, and they call him shit names, like Prospero and Miranda and Stephano and Trinculo did, and they poke him with sticks to make him snarl and curse, and they laugh at him. Plus they feed him crap food. So after a while of this he gets a bunch of diseases – he's never been vaccinated, right? – and one day he comes out in spots and a fever, and then he flops over and dies.'

Silence in the room. It's all too plausible.

'But that was too dark for us,' says Leggs. 'Why should the other ones in this play get a second chance at life, but not him? Why's he have to suffer so much for being what he is? It's like he's, you know, black or Native or something. Five strikes against him from Day One. He never asked to get born.'

More nods. Leggs has the audience. Where's he taking them? Felix wonders. Somewhere strange, you can see it in his eyes. He's about to spring a surprise. 'So here's what we're thinking,' says Leggs. 'We're thinking about that line, said by Prospero: "This thing of darkness I acknowledge mine." What's he mean by it? Just that Caliban works for him or is, like, his slave? It's gotta be more than that.' He leans forward, making eye contact, then more eye contact. 'This is what we think. It's gotta be true. Here it is: *Prospero is Caliban's dad.*'

Murmurings, small head-shakings. They aren't convinced. 'Stick with me,' says Leggs. 'Let's walk it through. His mom is a sorceress, right? Sycorax. She's wicked! Prospero is a sorcerer. They do a lot of the exact same kind of things – charms, spells, changing the weather – including putting the twist on Ariel, except that Prospero does those things better, and we're supposed to think it's okay for him but evil for her. Suppose they met earlier at, like, a sorcerer type of convention, and they had a thing together. One-night stand. He knocks her up, skedaddles back to Milan; she's up the spout, she gets caught, they dump her on the island.

'Prospero washes up onshore. Sycorax is dead by then, but he takes one look at Caliban and he knows right away whose kid this has to be. He slangs the dead mother, that's natural; he doesn't own up to the kid, but thinks he might make something of him anyway – the kid must have some good qualities, right, because it's half his. Proud of him at first, because Caliban's self-reliant, knows his way around the island, comes up with food, pig-nuts and fish, whatever – eager to please. So Prospero humours the kid, teaches him stuff. Language, and that.

'But then the kid takes a crack at Miranda. That's natural too, maybe not nice, was there consent, who knows, he said she said, but whose fault was it anyway, letting Miranda prance around in full view? Prospero should'a seen it coming. Should'a locked her up, if it was that important. Prospero ought to eat some of the blame for that number.

'But that's not what he does. Instead he gets in a twist, piles on the insults, starts with the tortures, overlooks the good points Caliban's got, such as musical talent. But by the end, Prospero's learning that maybe not everything is somebody else's fault. Plus, he sees that the bad in Caliban is pretty much the same as the bad in him, Prospero. They're both angry, both name-callers, both full of revenge: they're joined at the hip. Caliban is like his bad other self. Like father, like son. So he owns up: "This thing of darkness I acknowledge mine." That's what he says, and that's what he means.

'So after the play, Prospero tries to make up for what he did wrong. He takes Caliban onto the ship, runs him under the shower, scrubs off that fishy smell, orders him some fancy new clothes, makes him, like, a pageboy or something, so he can learn to eat from a plate. Says he's sorry and they need to start fresh. Appeals to the artistic side of Caliban, what with the beautiful dreams and all. Once Caliban is cleaned up and well dressed and has manners, people don't think he's ugly any more. They think he's, like, rugged.

'So Prospero sets him up as a musician, back in Milan. Once he gets a break, the kid does really well. He can bring out, like the darkness emotions in people, but in a musical way. He has to keep away from the booze though, it's poison to him, turns him crazy. So he makes the effort, and he stays clean.

'Next thing you know he's a star. Prospero's really proud of him. The kid is top billing at all the duke-type concerts. He's got a stage name, he's got a band: HAG-SEED AND THE THINGS OF DARKNESS. He's, like, world-famous.

'That's our report. We hope you like it.'

This time the class is in full agreement. There's a chorus of 'Yeahs' and 'Way-to-gos,' and a round of applause that swells to a rhythmic clapping, then a stamping of feet. 'Hag-Seed! Hag-Seed! We want Hag-Seed!'

Felix stands up. This shouldn't get too far out of control. 'That was excellent, Team Hag-Seed. Full marks! A very creative interpretation! And a fitting end to the formal part of this class. Next up, cast party! Are we ready?'

The bags of potato chips and the cans of ginger ale are handed out. There's talk, the clinking of ginger ale cans, an air of muted celebration. In a few minutes they'll sidle up to Felix one by one and cough up some form of bashful thanks. It's what happens at these parties, every time. That, plus the opening of the chip bags and the swift pocketing of the cigarettes.

The number of cigarettes in each bag is the same, and why not? They've all done so well. Once Felix is out of sight, the bargaining and trading will begin: cigarettes are an unofficial currency, desirable for bribes and the obtaining of goods and favours.

'Not my usual brand,' says Bent Pencil. Chuckles: everyone knows he doesn't smoke.

'If there's a hole in one end and fire at the other, I smoke it,' says Red Coyote.

Shiv: 'You're talking about my woman.' Laughter.

'Yeah, but which end is which?' More laughter. 'Sorry, Anne-Marie.'

'Watch it,' says Anne-Marie. 'Don't forget, I've got that goddess power.'

'By the way, well done, Anne-Marie,' says Felix. 'I didn't see that coming.'

'You always say magic should be unpredictable,' says Anne-Marie. 'I wanted to surprise you.'

'And you did,' says Felix.

'We're really grateful to you. Me and Freddie. It's –'

'No need for gratitude,' says Felix. 'I was pleased to help out.'

'We got a surprise for you too,' says Leggs, who has ambled over to join them.

'Oh?' says Felix. 'What kind of surprise?'

'It's an extra number we wrote,' says Leggs. 'Me and the Hag-Seeds. We all wrote it together. We're working on, like, a musical.'

'A musical?' says Anne-Marie. 'About Caliban?'

'Yeah, about what happens after the play's over. Doing that report got us thinking: why shouldn't Caliban have a play to himself?'

'Go on,' says Felix.

'Okay, so, it begins at the part where Stephano and Trinculo put him in a cage and show him off for money. But in the musical, he gets out of the cage. That's this number we did – where he gets out, and he says he's not doing any more slave work or living in a cage.'

Boom boom boom, the Hag-Seeds start the beat. Leggs chants:

Freedom, high-day! High-day, freedom! Freedom,
  high-day, freedom!
Got outta my cage, now I'm in a rage –
No more dams I'll make for fish,
Nor fetch in firing
At requiring,
Nor scrape trenchering, nor wash dish;
Ain't gonna any more lick your feet
Or walk behind you on the street,
Ain't gonna get on the back of the bus,
And you can give our land right back to us!

Ban-ban, Ca-Caliban,
Don't need no master, I am not your man!
So stuff it up your hole, gimme back what you stole,
Tellin' you it's late, I'm fillin' up with rage,
I'm gettin' all set to go on a ram-page!
Ain't gonna work for less than minimum wage –
Live in a shack and piss in a pail,
You earn yourself money by puttin' me in jail!

You kick me in the head, you dump me in the snow,
Leave me there for dead,

Freedom, high-day!
High-day, freedom!
Freedom, high-day,
freedom!

'Cause I'm nothin' to you.
Ban, ban, Ca-Caliban,
You think I'm an animal, not even a man!

Now Hag-Seed's black and Hag-Seed's brown,
Hag-Seed's red, don't care if you frown,
Hag-Seed's yellow and Hag-Seed's trash white,
He goes by a lotta names, he's roamin' in the night,
You treated him bad, now he's a sackful of fright,
Hag-Seed!

Ban, ban, Ca-Caliban,
Don't need no master, I am *not* your man!
Move it, man! Let it go, let it flow –
Don't need no, need no, need no! No no no!

'That's powerful,' says Felix. 'Very powerful.'

'More than powerful!' says Anne-Marie. 'It's got – it could be really – But what happens after he escapes from the cage?'

'We figure he might go after everyone who used to treat him in such a bad way,' says Leggs. 'Do a whole revenge thing, sort of like Rambo. Pick them off one by one, beginning with Stephano and Trinculo.'

'What about Prospero?' says Felix.

'And Miranda?' says Anne-Marie.

'Maybe they're not in the musical,' says Leggs. 'Or maybe they are. Maybe Caliban forgives them. Maybe he doesn't. Maybe stalks them, jumps them, goes to work with his claws. We're still working on it.'

Felix is intrigued: Caliban has escaped the play. He's escaped from Prospero, like a shadow detaching itself from its body and skulking off on its own. Now there's no one to restrain him. Will Prospero be spared, or will retribution climb in through his window one dark night and cut his weasand? Felix wonders. Gingerly, he feels his neck.

'Think you'd maybe direct it, Mr. Duke?' says Leggs. 'When we get it done? You'd be, like, our first choice.' He smiles shyly.

'If I'm still alive,' says Felix. He's absurdly pleased by the offer, though of course this will never happen. Or will it? 'It's possible. You never know.'

Acknowledgements

With thanks to the *Guardian*, where the essay 'We Are Double-Plus Unfree' was first published in 2015.

© Liam Sharp

MARGARET ATWOOD is one of the world's most celebrated writers and critics. Born in Canada in 1939, she has written over 70 books, among them prize-winning novels *The Blind Assassin*, *Cat's Eye*, *Alias Grace* and *The Heart Goes Last*, acclaimed poetry, short stories and non-fiction, books for children and a graphic novel.

She addresses the theme of humanity's freedom, or lack thereof, throughout her work, most notably in the internationally bestselling *The Handmaid's Tale*. First published in 1985, the novel saw a marked resurgence upon the election of Donald Trump as US President in 2016. It was adapted into an Emmy Award-winning TV series of the same name in 2017. About its origins, Atwood has said: 'One of my rules was that I would not put any events into the book that had not already happened in what James Joyce called the "nightmare" of history, nor any technology not already available. No imaginary gizmos, no imaginary laws, no imaginary atrocities. God is in the details, they say. So is the devil.'

Margaret Atwood was the first contributor to the Future Library with her book *Scribbler Moon*. The manuscript lies buried in a Norwegian forest and will be published in 2115. She is an outspoken activist for human rights and environmental causes and she and her partner, the writer Graeme Gibson, are Joint Honorary Presidents of the Rare Bird Society.

RECOMMENDED BOOKS BY MARGARET ATWOOD:

Hag-Seed
Alias Grace
The Heart Goes Last

VINTAGE MINIS

The Vintage Minis bring you some of the world's greatest writers on the experiences that make us human. These stylish, entertaining little books explore the whole spectrum of life – from birth to death, and everything in between. Which means there's something here for everyone, whatever your story.

Desire	Haruki Murakami
Love	Jeanette Winterson
Marriage	Jane Austen
Babies	Anne Enright
Language	Xiaolu Guo
Motherhood	Helen Simpson
Fatherhood	Karl Ove Knausgaard
Summer	Laurie Lee
Jealousy	Marcel Proust
Sisters	Louisa May Alcott
Home	Salman Rushdie
Race	Toni Morrison
Liberty	Virginia Woolf
Swimming	Roger Deakin
Friendship	Rose Tremain
Work	Joseph Heller
Money	Yuval Noah Harari
Austerity	Yanis Varoufakis
Injustice	Richard Wright
War	Sebastian Faulks
Depression	William Styron
Drinking	John Cheever

Eating	Nigella Lawson
Rave	Irvine Welsh
Psychedelics	Aldous Huxley
Calm	Tim Parks
Dreams	Sigmund Freud
Ghosts	M. R. James
Freedom	Margaret Atwood
Death	Julian Barnes